BY VINCE SPEZZANO
...from paperboy to president of USA Today

**Cover and cartoons by
Jim "GOOT" Guttenberg**

This book is dedicated to the memory
of my mother and father whose sense
of humor made growing-up fun.

ISBN: 1-878398-05-9

Blue Note Books
(407) 799-2583, FAX (407) 799-1942
1-800-624-0401

Printed in the United States of America

The Contents

Allen H. Neuharth, Founder *USA TODAY*

Foreword

Vince makes you laugh and cry. His book of jokes will liven up your conversations from the living room to the boardroom to the barroom.

— **Al Neuharth**

About The Author

MEET VINCE SPEZZANO

Who is Vince Spezzano, and how did he amass such a collection of humor? Vincent Edward Spezzano retired May 1991 as chairman of both the Gannett Rochester Newspapers and *Florida TODAY*, after 36 years with Gannett Company, Inc.

A native of Retsof, New York (a village near Rochester), he served as a U.S. Navy volunteer during World War II before pursuing higher education. He earned his B.A. in Journalism and English at Syracuse University, following two years of study in civil engineering.

His newspaper career ranged from paperboy to top management. Spezzano's second newspaper job was on the weekly newspaper, *Livingston Republican*, in

Geneseo, New York (the first, of course, was as a youthful paperboy). Hired as a police reporter for the *Lynchburg Daily News*, he moved from Lynchburg, Virginia to St. Louis, Missouri and the *Globe-Democrat* as a general reporter. From there, he made the jump to the Gannett Company, hired as a reporter on *The Times-Union* in Rochester.

He moved steadily upward in his career with Gannett...from police reporter to political columnist, from public service director to senior vice president of communications, on to President of *USA TODAY* and *USA Today International*. He also served as a Gannett Company director and headed the task force that developed the concept for *USA TODAY*.

He has twice been nominated for Pulitzer Prizes and has received countless honors and awards, including: the Silver Shovel of the International Newspaper Promotion Assn.; twice honored as Citizen of the Year in Rochester, New York; Communicator of the Year; and, was confirmed to the Order of the Cavaliere (Knight) from Italy.

He has been listed in *Who's Who in America* for nearly two decades and also is listed in *Who's Who in The East, in the South, Finance and Industry, and International Businessmen*.

A myriad of volunteer positions, both professionally and in community service, have honed his speaking skills. Spezzano has been a speaker and master of ceremonies in the USA, Canada, Mexico, Europe, Japan and at a dozen colleges and universities before audiences ranging in size from nine to 7,000.

Over the years as a guest speaker, he has compiled an enormous collection of humor. It is not unusual, even now in his retirement, to get an urgent call from someone needing jokes, anecdotes or truisms to "break the ice", "hook the audience", or make an effective closing for "their" speech.

At 70 years of age, he is the father of two sons and a daughter. He lives in Cocoa Beach, Florida with his wife, Marjorie Elliott Spezzano. Active in community service, he serves on seven community boards. He fills his leisure hours with golf, tennis, an occasional newspaper column and is presently working on a novel about the media world and its people.

Preface

As a speaker for most of my 35 years in the newspaper business (in positions ranging from reporter to President of *USA Today*), I was always looking for light material to help the heavy stuff go down.

This book has been produced for people who are looking for ideas – light material to help the heavy stuff go down and to get and hold their audience's attention. In it can be found ideas: jokes, ancedotes and truisms that they can use in business, in everyday life and for their enjoyment.

It was produced by hundreds who have contributed humor or wisdom (whether they knew I was listening or not).

Over the years I've been writing down most of the jokes I've heard and I've collected some of the best.

My 70th birthday prompted me to dig into my computer, desk drawers and files, and get them organized into categories. I'm hoping you'll find something for every occasion.

My thanks to My Friend Marge, My Artist Goot, His Friend Charlotte, who made this book possible, all My Friends – and everybody else.

Al Neuharth

■ A book becomes a classic when people who haven't read it begin to say they have.

■ A writer. Many of his articles have appeared in every major birdcage in the country.

■ Every day he makes two lists. One is a list of things to do and the other a list of who he's going to do it to.

■ He calls Dial-A-Prayer to see if there were any messages.

I worship the water he walks on.

- He doesn't lose his temper. He knows exactly where to find it.
- Humble. You don't have to call him sir. Kneeling is enough.
- Important. When he calls dial a prayer, he doesn't get a recording.
- No heart problem. He had one put in.
- Please don't make a fuss over him. Treat him like any emperor.
- Price of success - ulcers, high blood pressure, hypertension, nervous tics. People who work with him, have them all.
- Secure you will not be replaced by a robot. Impossible to make a robot that grovels.
- Someone said, God help us, and he said: "I'll try."
- The trouble with some self-made men is that they worship their creator.
- Very busy but always has time to listen to our problems — and add to them.
- Woman came out of book store with Al's book and a dictionary. Al said: Would you like me to autograph it? Woman said: Which one?

Airplanes

■ Airline attendants seem to be getting older and older. On my flight here, the stewardess told me *how* much fun it was working with Orville and Wilbur.

■ I always travel by bus. I have nothing against planes — but I've never heard of a bus running out of gas — and falling up.

■ I had a flight canceled recently, but the airline was very accommodating; they offered to lose my luggage on a later trip.

■ I was on a fast plane. It traveled faster than the speed of luggage.

■ I was on an old plane. You know how they name planes — 747, 727, 757. Mine was called 7.

■ If airline fares keep dropping, I may eventually be able to visit some of the cities where my luggage goes.

■ If God had meant man to fly, He would have made it easier to get to the airport.

■ Most airlines are assigned an air route; this airline was assigned to stay on a dirt road.

■ Orville Wright was on the first flight and arrived two days ahead of his baggage.

■ Pilot said he was flying a Boeing 7&7.

■ We'll soon be able to go clear around the world in

two hours — one hour flying and the other to get to the airport.

■ Columbus didn't have an easy time of it. He had to sail thousands of miles on uncharted seas, battling wind, and the fear of the unknown. On the other hand, he didn't have to change ships in Atlanta.

■ Columbus discovered America, after he made three more trips to the New World. He must have been trying to rack up those Frequent Explorer Bonus Miles.

Business

■ A big corporation becomes big because it gives service. When it ceases to do so, it gets small again.
■ A company is known by the people it employs.
■ A customer with a problem solved, will produce three

He's a big gun in the industry. He's been fired 12 times.

times the revenue of a customer without a problem.

■ An American shoe manufacturer sent two salesmen to Australia to get business among aborigines. One sent a telegram: "No business here. Natives don't wear shoes." Other sent: "Great opportunity here — natives don't wear shoes."

■ A merit pay raise means you're doing well. An annual pay raise means you're doing time.

■ A perfect advertisement is one that makes people glad they bought.

■ A successful seminar depends on the ratio of thinking to drinking and meeting to eating.

■ A word of encouragement during a failure is worth more than a whole book of praises after a success.

■ After all is said and nothing is done, the committee meeting is over.

■ Air travel these days is great — especially for those people who aren't in a hurry.

■ Airline ads, hotel ads, and insurance policies have a lot in common. The big type giveth and the small type taketh away.

■ An advertising agency is 85% confusion and 15% commission. – *Fred Allen*

■ An Arab Sheik on tour, stopped for an apple at a stand. The farmer said apples cost $50. The Sheik said apples must be scarce. The farmer said he had many apples but he was scarce of sheiks.

■ From Gen. Eisenhower on leadership: Put a string on a table. Pull and it will follow wherever you wish.

Push it and it will go nowhere at all.
- Be positive, except if you are positive you cannot sell someone, then you are negative.
- Being right. There's only one substitute for being right; being the boss.
- Ben Franklin may have discovered electricity, but it was the man who invented the meter who made the money.
- Business has taught me that sales meetings aren't needed when there are sales.
- Business is always interfering with pleasure – but it makes other pleasures possible.
- Business is so bad, we've just made the Misfortune 500.
- Cemetery director: I have a lot of people under me, but nobody listens.
- Chinese word for "crisis" is composed of two picture characters...one meaning "danger" and the other meaning "opportunity".
- Closed suggestion box: The handle was broken and it wouldn't flush.
- Company in bankruptcy is permitted to continue to do things that got them in trouble in the first place.
- Company president memo to personnel manager: "Search the organization for an alert, aggressive young man who could step into my shoes — and fire him."
- Conference is where a guy with the smallest idea and the biggest mouth gets the most attention.

- Creditors have better memories than debtors. – *Ben Franklin*
- The customer at Nordstrom's is always right. A customer marched in with a tire and told the salesman he was dissatisfied. The salesman gave the man the refund. He didn't tell him that Nordstrom's does not sell tires.
- Don't fix the blame; fix the problem.
- Don't just make good decisions. Make decisions good.
- Don't learn the tricks of the trade. Learn the trade.
- Eat, drink and be merry for tomorrow your accountant will explain the new tax law to you.
- The economy was so bad, a man was laid off, and he was self-employed.
- Educators and employers look at things differently. To an educator, an MBA is a Master of Business Administration. To an employer, an MBA is a Moderately Bright Accountant.
- Every man is presumed innocent unless he just came back from a convention.
- Everyone needs long-range goals, if for no other reason than to keep from being frustrated by short-range failures.
- Experience is what enables you to recognize a mistake when you make it again.
- Failure is never fatal and success is never final.
- Financial officers: They come in after the battle and shoot the wounded.
- Getting to the top is like getting to the top of a tree –

you can climb up the tree…or you can sit on an acorn.

■ Good salesmen are hard to find. Last week I had to call three bars, two movie houses and a massage parlor to find one.

■ Good supervision is the art of getting average people to do superior work.

■ Have you noticed that as soon as you find the key to success they change the locks?

■ He that cannot obey, cannot command. – *Ben Franklin*

■ He who hesitates is bossed.

■ He who works with his hands is a laborer. He who works with his hands and his head is a craftsman. He who works with his hands, head and heart is an artist. He who works with his hands, and his head and his heart and his feet is a salesman.

■ Hens make money while sitting down. Salesmen don't!

■ Hiring a consultant is like hiring a plane spotter the day after Pearl Harbor.

■ Honesty is the best policy. But remember, it's not the only policy.

■ How would you feel if your boss gave you a new appointment book and it only went up to May?

■ I don't get the feeling that I'm moving up the corporate ladder. I feel more like I'm walking under it.

■ I never give them hell. I just tell them the truth and they think it's hell. – *Harry Truman*

■ I won't say this is a tough place to work but last week six people quit to become slaves.

■ If a customer has a good experience, he'll tell three

other people. If he has had a bad experience, he'll tell 10 other people.

- If at first you do succeed, try something harder.
- If at first you don't succeed, don't take any more stupid chances.
- If at first you don't succeed, don't show up in the morning.
- If at first you don't succeed, you'll get a lot of advice.
- If at first you don't succeed, start checking the help-wanted ads.
- If my boss calls, get his name.
- If the cake is bad, what good is the frosting.
- If you aren't fired with enthusiasm, you will be fired with enthusiasm. - *Vince Lombardi*
- If you don't know where you are going, any road will get you there.
- If you find a path with no obstacles on it, the chances are that it doesn't lead anywhere.
- In my company we call it the petty cash fund. The boss calls it payroll.
- In the race for quality, there is no finish line. – *David Kearns,* CEO Xerox
- In this age of workaholics, I've never seen so many on the wagon.
- It takes months to find a customer; seconds to lose one.
- It's amazing how much permanent confusion can be caused by a temporary secretary.
- It's better to wear-out than to rust-out.

- Jet lag is when your briefcase arrives a day ahead of your brain.
- Leadership is action, not position.
- Making excuses doesn't change the truth.
- Men do not fail; they give up trying.
- Millions of Americans aren't working — but thank God, they've got jobs.
- Monday isn't a day — It's a condition.
- Most people like hard work. Particularly when they are paying for it.
- It's much more dignified to say we're moving in cycles rather than running in circles.
- My company was having trouble choosing a consulting firm so we hired a consultant to help us.
- My supervisor found a way to keep an eye on our main competitor — he went to work for them.
- New corporate policy: Salary increases will become effective just as soon as you do.
- Nobody will ever get ahead of you as long as he is kicking you in the seat of the pants.
- No matter what happens, I never make any trouble at airports. I'm an innocent standby.
- Nobody ever listened himself out of a job. – *Calvin Coolidge*
- It's not whether you win or lose but how you place the blame.
- Of all intellectual faculties, judgment is the last to mature.
- Old accountants never die; they just lose their bal-

ance.

- Only the customer decides how big a company will be.
- Only the lead dog has a change in scenery.
- Our sales department likes our product so well, they hate to part with it.
- Persistence. A salesman visited the office of a tough customer and was let in just before 5 p.m. The man said: "You ought to feel honored. I've refused to see 12 salesmen." Salesman said: "I know — I'm them."
- Personally, I don't believe in this concept of dressing for success. Face it. Can anyone here tell me what color necktie Moses was wearing when he parted the Red Sea?
- Plans will get you into things but you have got to work your way out. — *Will Rogers*
- Postal third class: Strapped on the back of an insane person who wanders aimlessly throughout America.
- A promising exec at IBM was involved in a risky venture that lost $10 million. His boss called him in. The exec said he assumed he would want his resignation. The boss said no, "We just spent $10 million educating you."
- Research is cheap if you want to stay in business, expensive if you don't.
- Retailer 1: My business went under because of too much advertising. Retailer 2: But you never spent anything on advertising. Retailer 1: I know, but my competitor did.

- Salesmen: If their lips move, they are lying.
- Second best is okay, unless everyone else is tied for first.
- Service: In order to be successful, we must sell our goods at a profit and still satisfy our customers. If we satisfy the customer but fail to get the profit, we will soon be out of business. If we get the profit but fail to satisfy the customer, we will soon be out of customers. The secret of doing both lies in one word *service*. Service means doing something so valuable for the customer that he is glad to pay a price that allows us to make a profit.
- A small store had many bags of salt. A man said: You certainly must sell a lot of salt. Grocer: I can't sell salt at all. But the guy who sells me the salt — he can sell salt!
- Some folks aren't hard of hearing; they're hard of listening.
- Some people think the way to stay out of trouble is to stay out of sight.
- Stores having two for one sales: For every two dollars spent, you get one dollar's value.
- Strange how unimportant a job is when you are asking for a raise, and how important when you want to take the day off.
- Succeed: All you have to do to be successful is follow the advice you give to others.
- Success is doing what you like to do and making a living at it.

- Success is like a river. To stay strong, it must keep moving. If it stops, it stagnates.
- Success is not money, power and position. Success is the warm feeling you get when you have money, power and position.
- Success: If at first you do succeed — try to hide your astonishment.
- Ten characteristics of a good leader 1. Persistence (not insistence); 2. Imagination; 3. Vision; 4. Sincerity; 5. Integrity; 6. Poise; 7. Thoughtfulness; 8. Common sense; 9. Altruism (lives by Golden Rule); 10. Initiative.
- The best executive is the one who has sense enough to pick good men to do what he wants done, and self-restraint enough to keep from meddling with them while they do. — *Theodore Roosevelt*
- The best thinking has been done in solitude. The worst has been done in turmoil. – *Thomas Edison*
- The boss is into exercise. When you ask for a raise, he tells you to take a walk.
- The difference between a career and a job is about 20 hours a week.
- The higher you go, the more dependent you become on others.
- The man who removes a mountain begins by carrying away small stones. - *Chinese Proverb*
- The man who rows the boat, doesn't have time to rock it.
- The salmon always was pink fish, until fishermen found

the white salmon. The white salmon fishermen guaranteed to the public that salmon turned pink in the can.

■ The only thing worse than having a boss is being a boss.

■ The only time you don't want to fail is the last time you try.

■ The person who knows how, has a job, the person who knows why, is the boss.

■ The phone company has us by the bills.

■ The will to succeed is important but it isn't worth a nickel unless you also have the will to prepare.

■ Never trust a man who doesn't worry.

■ Three men with adjacent businesses in same building: At one end, the businessman put up a sign, "Year-End Clearance." At other end, the owner put up sign, "Closing-Out Sale." The businessman in the middle put up sign, "Main Entrance."

■ To err is human, to forgive is against company policy.

■ To err is human — and to blame it on a computer is even more so.

■ To get employees to come to work on time, a Michigan company provides 45 parking spaces for 50 cars.

■ To get something done, a committee should consist of no more than three men, two of them absent.

■ To think too long about doing a thing often becomes its undoing. — *Eva Young*

■ Today's sales should be better than yesterday's — but not better than tomorrow's.

■ Try means nothing. Try standing. You either stand

up or fall down.
- Trying times are times for trying.
- Two movers struggled with a crate in the doorway. One said: "We'll never get this in." The other guy said: "In? I thought we were trying to get it out."
- Ulcers show you care.
- An unbreakable comb broke. Salesman said: "And this is how it looks from the inside."
- Unless morale improves, the firing will continue.
- We all know that the earth is not flat-broke – yet.
- We have a top notch sales force. Too bad we don't sell top notches.
- We're not in this to test the waters. We're in this to make waves.
- What salespeople sell…is people.
- When I bought my car, the dealer assured me it was a bargain that wouldn't last long. He was right.
- Try not to become a man of success but rather try to become a man of value. – *Albert Einstein.*
- True that Einstein discovered $E = MC^2$… but could he program a VCR?
- We would not need a machine to do the work of 50 people if 50 people did the work of 50 people.
- I came home from the office and I said to my wife: "Remember when we first got married and you said there would be no such thing as my troubles or your troubles, just our troubles? She said: "Yes." I said: "Our secretary is pregnant!"
- Everybody is trying to economize. Remember Snow

White? She just laid off three Dwarfs.

■ When one door closes, another opens; but we often look so long and so regretfully upon the closed door that we do not see the one which has opened for us.
– *Alexander Graham Bell*

■ When you're through changing, you're through.

■ You are either in the parade or watching it.

■ You can't be afraid of stepping on toes if you want to go dancing.

■ I'll tell you what kind of an office I work in. I have a computer with ulcers.

■ New York is where cab drivers know everything about politics, everything about economics, everything about life and love and sex — everything but the shortest way from the airport.

■ Santa Claus spends a year trying to find out who was naughty and nice. Any secretary could tell him in a minute.

■ Didn't quite make it: Give Me Liberty or Forget It... Leave it to Woodchuck... Crime and Probation... Burger Duke... Romeo and Julie... Sesame Avenue... Ben Him – *Steve Lawhead* in *Campus Life*

■ Linemen in pioneer days could put up telephone poles any where. A farmer ordered one off his land. The lineman showed the farmer a paper giving him right to put a pole anyplace. At that time a hugh ferocious bull charged across the field. As the farmer ran to the fence, he shouted: "Doesn't do any good to show me that paper, show it to the bull."

My boss is a fine example of a bad example.

Bosses

■ Asking my boss for a raise is like asking the Venus di Milo for her autograph.

■ Before you have an argument with your boss, take a good look at both sides — his side and the outside.

■ The boss isn't a go-getter. He's more like a YOU-go-getter.

■ A boss put up sign that said: "Do It Now." The results: The treasurer had skipped out with $50,000, the head bookkeeper had eloped with his secretary, three salesmen demanded raises and a boy in the mailroom had gone out West to become a movie producer.

■ Boss to personnel director: My son needs a job. He's your new assistant but do not show him favoritism. Treat him just as you would any other son of mine.

■ During a sales meeting, the manager was berating the sales staff for low sales figures. "If a football team isn't winning, the players are released — right?" Quarterback said: "If the whole team was having trouble we usually got a new coach."

■ Hard man to reach. When I call him at the office, he puts me on hold. When I call his car phone, he puts me on idle.

■ His policy: If you're well enough to call in sick, you're well enough to come to work.

■ I don't want any yes-men around me. I want everybody to tell me the truth, even if it costs them their jobs.

■ I lost my job at the orange juice factory. The boss said I couldn't concentrate.

■ I recently attended a stress management seminar and discovered it's management that causes stress.

■ I'd still be at my last job if it weren't for my boss's tone of voice. I didn't like the way he said: "You're fired."

■ My boss bawled me out for being late. I confessed that I overslept. He said, "What! You sleep at home, too?"

■ My boss told me my work was improving, and if I keep it up, he'd release my family.

■ My boss was his own worst enemy — then he hired me.

■ Surprise tour: The boss noticed a young man leaning against a packing crate. He angrily asked what he was paid a week? The man said $200. The boss paid him and told him to get out. The boss asked the manager, who the young man was and was told he didn't work here. He was delivering a package.

- The boss called me into his office to tell me he's confident in me – confident that I will be able to find another job.
- The boss doesn't like yes-men. He wants us to always tell him the truth, no matter how badly it might hurt us.
- The boss is a year away from being an exceptional leader. Next year he'll be two years away.
- The boss is against maternity benefits. He says if we offer maternity benefits, every Tom, Dick and Harry will get pregnant.
- The boss is even tempered. He's angry all the time.
- The boss is very talented. At a recent office party, he performed his human being impression.
- The boss knows exactly where he's going and where he's been. He just doesn't know where he is.
- The boss told me I was in line for a promotion – the end of the line to be precise.
- There's no limit to what the boss can do if he puts someone else's mind to it.
- We pitched in and bought the boss a birthday present – a Dr. Kervorkian gift certificate.
- When all else fails, try the boss's suggestion.
- When it comes to business, the boss has a sixth sense. Too bad he's missing the first five.

Closing

The fat lady hasn't sung, but it's over anyway.

- Anyone else have something to say before we adjourn this century?
- If I've gotten my message across, it's my hope that some of you will leave here inspired. The rest of you will at least wake-up refreshed.
- Orange juice without vodka, is like a day without sunshine.
- And in conclusion, I'd like to stop talking.
- I could go on and on – and I think I just did.
- I promise to answer all of your questions if you will accept all of my answers.
- I see that my time has run out — along with a good part of my audience.
- I want to congratulate you on that fantastic display of terminal talent.
- I'd like to end my speech with this piece of advice: Never end a speech with a piece of advice.
- In closing, I'd like to say TGIF – Thank God I'm Finished.
- In conclusion, permit me to paraphrase Shakespeare, "All's well that ends.."
- Our soldiers are returning home — and now all of you can do the same.
- That's about it. Please try not to hurt anyone as you make your mad dash for the exits.
- Famous last words: George Custer - "Oh yeah? You and what army?"... Magellan – "See you around."...Julius Caesar – "Ouch"... Count Dracula - "Good Morning."

- Mrs. Armstrong: "Neil has no more business taking flying lessons than the man in the moon."
- Mrs. Morse: "Sam, stop tapping your fingers on the table."
- Mrs. Washington "George never did have a head for money."
- On to Little Big Horn for glory, we've caught them napping. – *Gen. George Custer*

Country Songs

■ Baby, I may not be Elvis, but at least I ain't dead.
■ Don't treat me like a stranger just because we've never met.
■ I gave her a ring and she gave me the finger.

The family reunion ain't no place to meet girls.

Darlin', if you loved me, you'd wash my truck.

- I'd have made it to the altar but my bail was set too high.
- I'm a handkerchief woman in a Kleenex world.
- If she wasn't so good looking, I might have seen the train.
- If you really loved me, you would have married someone else.
- If you're bad enough for the city jail, you're good enough for me.
- It's a crime to love a cop if he's married.
- Someone up there must love you, cause no one down here does.

Definitions

- A colleague is someone called in at the last minute to share the blame.
- A conference is a gathering of important people who singly can do nothing, but together decide that nothing can be done. — *Fred Allen*
- A conservative is a liberal who's been mugged.
- A consultant is a kibitzer who charges.
- *A* diamond is forever, meaning that it takes that long

Luxuries are what other people buy.

to pay it off.

- A diamond is just a piece of coal that made good under pressure.
- A friend is a person who knows you and still likes you.
- A friend in need is a friend to avoid.
- A meeting is a place where people get together to talk about what they should already be doing.
- A meeting is when everything comes together but minds.
- A panel is four people, each wondering why the others were picked.
- A parking place is an area that disappears while you are making a U-turn.
- A pessimist is an optimist who tried to practice what he preached.
- A proverb is a short sentence based on long experience.
- A reformer is a guy who rides through a sewer in a glass-bottomed boat.
- A true friend is someone who is there for you when he'd rather be anywhere else
- Adios: Spanish breakfast cereal.
- Alimony: When two people make a mistake and one person pays for it.
- Amnesia is nature's way of saying, forget it.
- An environmentalist is someone who writes a 600-page book asking where all the trees have gone.
- An orgy is no fault sex.
- Annie Oakleaf: Well-decorated Western sharpshooter.

- Antique: More than 50 years old and serves no useful purpose.
- Apathy: What do I think about it? I can take it or leave it
- Bachelor's diet: You only eat half of what you cook.
- Bad day is when your horn goes off accidentally and remains stuck as you follow a group of Hell's Angel bikers on the Freeway.
- Bad day is when your twin sister forgets your birthday.
- Bad day when you want to put on the clothes you wore home from last night's party — and there aren't any.
- Bad day when your wife wakes up feeling amorous — and you have a headache.
- Bankruptcy: The kiss of debt.
- Bankruptcy: The inability to repay debt or remember Swiss bank account numbers.
- Bore: When you ask him how he is, he tells you.
- Brigham Rung: Founder of the Church of the Ladder Day Saints.
- Bustghosters: Surgeons who still perform silicone breast implants but are afraid to reveal their names.
- Ciao: Italian puppy food.
- Cigarette's Anonymous: Someone comes by and you get drunk together.
- Claustrophobia: A Texan in Rhode Island.
- Confidence is the part of you that knows you've got what it takes, even when the IRS wants to take what

you got.

- Conscience is that still small voice that tells you what other people should do.
- Consultants are childless people who make a living telling others how to be parents.
- Courage is being scared to death and saddling up anyway. — *John Wayne*
- Creativity: Most of us have it but few of us use it.
- Cutter, gutter, butter. Name a boat, a moat and a goat.
- Diplomacy is to think twice before you don't say anything.
- Diplomacy is saying "nice dog, nice dog" until you find a rock.
- Duck Holliday — only known survivor of the O.K. Corral shoot-out.
- A dude ranch is just like playing house except there is a little more horsing around.
- Efficiency is doing things right. Effectiveness is doing the right thing. Doing the wrong thing efficiently is worse than useless. — *Peter Drucker*
- Efficient work is the combination of hard work and smart work.
- Egomaniacs suffer from delusions of adequacy.
- Excuses: 1. I forgot; 2. No one told me to go ahead; 3. I didn't think it was that important; 4. Wait until the boss comes back and ask him; 5. I didn't know you were in a hurry for it; 6. That's the way we've always done it; 7. That's not in my department; 8.

How was I to know this was different?; 9. I'm waiting for an O.K.; 10. That's his job - not mine.

■ Experience is a hard teacher. She gives the test first and the lesson afterwards.

■ Experience is that wonderful knowledge that enables you to recognize a mistake when you make it again.

■ Experience is what you get when you didn't get what you wanted. It's when you were expecting something else.

■ Failure is the path of least resistance.

■ Failures are divided into two classes: Those who thought and never did, and those who did and never thought.

■ Fast foods: Japanese - hurryyaki... Italian – pasta fazoom... Kosher – gefaste fish... Mexican – taco pronto.

■ Favorite charity— my wife's next husband.

■ Freedom is doing what you like. Happiness is liking what you do.

■ Frustration is not having anyone to blame but yourself.

■ Good breeding consists in concealing how much we think of ourselves and how little we think of the other person.

■ Good conversationalist is not one who remembers what was said but says what someone wants to remember.

■ Gourmet restaurants are where you over-pay to under eat.

- Gypsy Rose Lee Trevino: Only known professional golfer known to strip tees.
- Hooker Tee Washington: Educator and frustrated golfer.
- Hospitality is making your guests feel at home, even though you wish they were.
- Housework is something you do that nobody notices unless you don't do it.
- Hypocrite is someone who complains about too much sex and violence on the video tapes he rents.
- Ice cap: Bellhop at the Nome Hilton.
- Icicle: Bicycle built for me.
- Idol: Statue of imitations.
- If a man keeps his trap shut, the world will beat a path to his door.
- If it's fixed, don't work it.
- Ilk: A silk elk.
- Impeach: To charge a really nice guy with wrong-doing in office.
- Incur: To acquire an undesirable dog.
- Indy 500: Hoosier Social Register.
- Infrequent Flyer: Someone trying to get out.
- Irrigate: To annoy someone by dousing them with water.
- It's better to know nothing than to learn nothing. - *Talmud*
- Jeep: Sound made by military chickens.
- Jet Lag: The interval between scheduled and actual arrival of the airplane.

- Junk is something you keep and then throw away two weeks before you need it.
- Karate: Japanese diamond.
- Knowledge has never been known to enter the head via an open mouth.
- Leadership: It's the price of leadership to do the thing you believe has to be done at the time it must be done. - *Lyndon Johnson*
- Lee Iacocca acronym: "I Am Chairman of Chrysler Corporation (of) America.
- Little Red Robin Hood: She stole from the rich and gave to her poor grandmother.
- Loser: His family crest has an Edsel on it.
- Love is never having to say you tested positive.
- Luck is what enabled others to get where they are. Talent is what enabled us to get where we are.
- Memory is something that makes you aware of what you forgot to do.
- Mud puddle: Scene of the grime.
- Nostalgia is longing for a place you wouldn't move back to.
- Nostalgia is not what it used to be.
- Obstacles are those frightful things you see when you take your eyes off your goals.
- Opportunist: Someone who took the chance while you were still making up your mind.
- Optimists are people who get wealthy by buying out pessimists.
- Optimist invents the airplane and the pessimist in-

vents the parachute.

■ Overoptimism is waiting for your ship to come in when you haven't sent one out.

■ P.T.L. Barnum: Showman who said, "There's a sucker born again every minute."

■ Pandora's Rule: Never open a box you didn't close.

■ Paranoid: Wanted his coffin to lock from the inside.

■ Paul Reverse: Tory patriot who warned the British that the Americans were coming.

■ Perfect guest is a person who makes his host and hostess feel very much at home.

■ Perry Masson: Television lawyer who will solve no case before its time.

■ Poise is the ability to keep talking while the other guy picks up the check.

■ Pong, dong, kong. Name a ping, a ding and a king.

■ Power equals the weakness of others times their number.

■ Pride is something we have. Vanity is something others have.

■ Progress is a continuing effort to make the things we eat, drink and wear as good as they used to be.

■ Quandary: The predicament of someone in church who suddenly discovers he has nothing smaller than a 20 dollar bill.

■ RCA Victor Hugo: Inventor of the car radio and author of "The Hatchback of Notre Dame."

■ Recession is when the economy starts crumbling. A depression is when everybody realizes it.

- Redundant: Unexplained mystery, frozen ice cubes, dangerous menace, hollow tube, going to Buffalo to commit suicide, trained experts, positive benefits, silly nonsense.
- Self-confidence is when you believe you're right 100% of the time. Sometimes more.
- Silence is the most perfect expression of scorn. – *George B. Shaw*
- Silicone: It makes mountains out of molehills.
- Smart is when you believe only half of what you hear. Brilliant is when you know which half to believe.
- Sophie Trucker: Last of the red hot teamsters.
- Star Wars: The Academy Awards.
- Stress is the feeling you feel when you feel you're going to feel a feeling you feel you'd rather not feel.
- Stress: That confusion created when one's mind overrides the body's basic desire to choke the living shit out of some asshole who desperately needs it.
- Success depends partly on whether people like you wherever you go or whenever you go.
- Success is relative; the more success, the more relatives.
- Success is winning on purpose.
- Tact is changing the subject without changing your mind.
- Tact is the art of making a point without making an enemy.
- That's not a lie, it's a terminological inexactitude. – *Alexander Haig*

■ Talent is a flame. Genius is a fire.

■ The best way to know a man is to watch him when he is angry. – *Hebrew Proverb*

■ The biggest room in the world is the room for improvement.

■ The genius of modern technology lies in making things to last 50 years — and making them obsolete in three.

■ The measure of a creator is the amount of life he puts into his work. We measure…by the amount of work he puts into our life.

■ The powerful speak slowly, as if time were plentiful.

■ The real test of a polite person is to have the same ailment the other person is describing — and not mention it.

■ The ultimate definition of a sadist and a masochist. A sadist is a real estate broker who sells a house described as a "Handyman's Special." A masochist is the one who buys it.

■ Tradition is what you have when you're too lazy to think of something new.

■ Troublemaker is a guy who rocks the boat then persuades everyone else there is a storm at sea.

■ Unless you're the lead dog, the scenery never changes.

■ Unreliable: You can't depend on anyone to be wrong all the time.

■ Venetian Blind: Hiding place for an Italian duck.

■ Vincent Van Goo: Finger painter.

■ Vocation: a job at the beach.

■ WALLMARK: When you care enough to deface the

very best.
- What do you give a girl who has everything? Penicillin.
- Wit penetrates. Humor envelops.
- Work with some men is as besetting as sin?
- Yankee: To a foreigner, an American. To a Southerner, a Northerner. To a Northerner, he lives in New England. To a New Englander, someone from Vermont. To a Vermonter, someone who still uses an outhouse.
- Yuppie: Young Unemployed Professional.

Education

■ I'm not myself today, so things should go well.
■ A man applied for a banking job. The personnel manager asked him where he got his training. The man said: "At Yale." The personnel man said: "That's fine. Now, give me your full name." The man answered: "Yonny Yohnson."
■ A nanosecond is the time that separates the gradua-

Not a good student.
On his first day in school, he flunked bus.

tion ceremony from the alumni association's first financial appeal.

- A strange educational system when you find algebra taught in the fourth grade and spelling in college.
- As long as there are math tests, there will always be prayer in the schools.
- Commencement address – Price of a college education: "This college is an institution which prepares students for the real world." Senior in first row: "It sure as hell is. Right off the bat, I'm in debt $50,000."
- Education has changed since I went to school. In those days you didn't get credit for learning about sex, you got punished.
- Education is a weapon, whose effect depends on who holds it in his hands and at whom it is aimed. – *Joseph Stalin*
- Education is learning what you didn't even know you didn't know.
- Education will never become as expensive as ignorance.
- I found a way to beat the high costs of college. I persuaded my kid to drop out of high school.
- I have a parrot that has a better vocabulary than my son after two years in college.
- I have never let my schooling interfere with my education. — *Mark Twain*
- I'd like to be independent, but I can't do it alone.
- If a tree falls in the forest and no one is present, will environmentalists still make a noise?

- If two teenagers can breed in the back of a Volkswagen, why does it take 2,000 acres for the spotted owl to do the same thing?
- Illiteracy is nothing to write home about.
- In the first place God made idiots; this was for practice; then he made school boards. – *Mark Twain*
- Kids love school. It's graduating they're not too thrilled with.
- My kid is a terrible student The only reason he isn't left back is that his teachers are scared they'll get him again.
- My son said there was a food tampering scare in the school lunchroom. They found traces of meat in the hamburgers.
- Once enrolled in a relaxation class but slept through it.
- One school had so many dropouts, there's no alumni.
- Our school district has bought a computer that does everything a real teacher can do. Yesterday it went on strike.
- Personally, I approve of sex education in the schools. Teachers have to learn it somewhere.
- School so small that driver training and sex education were taught in the same car.
- September is that time when thousands of people kick, scream and cry because they have to go to school. They are the teachers.
- Teachers are people who used to like children.
- The graduation ceremony is where the speaker says:

"The future is in your hands," and he's talking to the same kids who throw your newspapers into the bushes.

■ The cost of college keeps rising. That's what they really mean by higher education.

■ The trouble with some people today is that they are educated beyond their intelligence.

■ These days, if you can afford to go to college, there's no need to go.

■ Three football players were caught studying in the library.

■ Truant officers today spend their time bringing back teachers.

■ TV today is educational – but only if you compare it to education today.

Ethnic Jokes

■ Jewish Boy Scouts motto: Buy insurance.

■ A protest in China is a lot like our protests, except an hour later you feel like protesting again.

■ Columbus claimed America for Spain. Two Indians said "Chi e Questo Patzo?" (Key a questo-patzo - Who is that crazy guy?)

Italian fast-food: Pasta fazoom.

51

- Czechoslovakian athlete was asked during an eye examination if he could read the bottom line. He replied, "Read it? I know him!"
- Eating Mexican food can give you a breath that will abort a cruise missile in mid-flight.
- Half German and half Polish. Hates Jews but doesn't know why.
- I have my faults. But being wrong ain't one of them.
  – Jimmy Hoffa
- Italian alzheimer: Forgets everything but grudges.
- Polish coyote: Chewed off three legs and still was caught in the trap.
- Voted for (...) because he's Italian? No. Because I'm Italian.
- What do you say to a man in a three piece suit? Will the defendant please rise.
- What's black, blue, floats in the river? People who tell Italian jokes.
- Why is a Chinese fortune cookie written in English?

Family

■ Active in community affairs — until his wife found out about it

■ Because of muggers, my wife insists I walk her mother home. It's ridiculous. What do I care what happens to muggers?

■ Dumb thing is training bra. What are you going to

I told my brother-in-law "my home is your home"
- so he sold it.

teach them?

- God could not be everywhere and therefore he made mothers. – *American proverb*
- Happiness is seeing your sister, brother-in-law, their three kids, two dogs and cat approaching your front door and you are seeing this in the rear-view mirror of your car.
- I have no luck — If my ship comes in, it'll probably be loaded with relatives.
- I'll take up camping when nature comes up with a bush that flushes.
- I'm a household name but only in my household.
- Large families are getting so expensive nowadays that only the poor can afford them.
- Loved to go to Grandma's house for Thanksgiving because she had what it takes to make the traditional Thanksgiving dinner — money.
- My shy family came over in the *Wallflower.*
- Now that we have indoor plumbing, we cook outdoors.
- Reading will: "And finally, to my cousin George, who always sat around and never did anything, but wanted to be remembered in my will, I want to say, "Hi, George.""
- Roots: Still put on a coat to go to the bathroom.
- The most important thing a father can do for his children is to love their mother.
- We didn't have a family tree. We had a family bush.
- We have the latest in security systems – two Dober-

mans and a mother-in-law.

■ We were so poor, burglars used to break in and leave things.

■ Wealth is a relative matter. The more wealth you have, the more relatives you hear from.

■ Express emotion: Play, Laugh and Touch each day.

Golf

■ A golf round which begins well, ends poorly. A golf
  round which begins poorly ends worse.
■ A new ball never makes it over the lake.
■ A putted ball does not listen to directions.
■ A putter guaranteed to take five strokes off a round
  will invariably add five.
■ A sandbagger and your money will soon join forces.

The official language of golf is profanity.

- Any difficult shot can be made impossible if enough time is taken to study it.
- Any golfer who says he plays just for the exercise lies about everything else, too.
- Every shot – good or bad – pleases someone.
- Friend showed off his great golf ball. Hit it in the woods and it starts beeping. In the water, it glows. In the sand, a little antenna comes up through the sand. I asked where he got it. He said, "I found it."
- Golf is like taxes. You work hard to get to the green, and then wind up in the hole.
- I'm being inducted into the PGA – The Pathetic Golfers Association.
- If it feels natural, you're doing it wrong.
- Just because you know what ails your game doesn't mean you can cure it.
- Long putts are a cinch when it's for a triple bogey.
- Never trust an 18 handicapper who carries a 1-iron in his bag.
- One percent of the distance is responsible for 90% of the strokes.
- OOPS is what an employee says to his boss when he makes a hole in one.
- Planning a golf match in advance makes bad weather inevitable.
- President Ford hit an eagle, a birdie, an elk and a moose.
- The best starting times are allotted to people who least deserve them.

- The best way to play golf is to keep one eye on the ball and the other eye on your opponent's arithmetic.
- The deal that was in the bag on the 9th will be in the rough by the 18th.
- The more you practice your good stroke, the worse it gets. The more you practice your weak stroke, the worse it gets.
- The player with the loudest clothes will have the highest score.
- The shorter the shot, the longer the excuse.
- The wetter the fairways, the more likelihood of a hole in your golf shoe.
- There is more to life than breaking par.
- Very competitive golfer missed a one foot putt. He broke his club, threw the ball in the woods, tossed his golf bag in the pond, grabbed a towel in clubhouse, knotted it around his neck, and hung himself from a steam pipe. Rest of his foursome come into locker room and one says to the strangling golfer, "You want to play tomorrow." The hanging man said: "What time?"

Government

■ A government is the only vessel known to leak from the top.

■ A typical Presidential press conference reminds me of Moses – an aged man comes down from the second floor with two 3 x 5 tablets on which are written the

Keep our city clean. Eat a pigeon.

Ten Confusions.

■ A scientist has invented a robot that does absolutely nothing. It may put thousands of Federal employees out of work.

■ Because of overcrowding, convicts should wait for a vacancy before committing their next crime.

■ Doctor told a Federal employee to take a long rest so he went back to work.

■ Government is like sex. The more you need, the less you get.

■ Government is too big and too important to be left to the politicians.

■ He has no right to make himself so small. He's not that big.

■ I wish they wouldn't say the pen is mightier than the sword. I'd hate to think of the post office as our first line of defense.

■ Modify the old sayings. Those who can, do. Those who can't still get paid.

■ Postal rates. 32 cents – 4 cents postage, 28 cents storage.

■ The post office has increased the cost of mailing a letter but look how much more time they spend delivering it.

■ Who else but the Army would issue you a duffel bag and then complain if your clothes are wrinkled.

■ There is a great deal of satisfaction in being a vice president. One advantage is you can take a two-hour lunch break without hindering sales.

Heckler

■ Are you done or have you stopped to come up for air?

■ Excuse me, sir, but I notice you're beginning to hesitate. A good sign. It means your brain is trying to make contact with your mouth.

■ Five minutes with you, Sir, and even the Pope would be pushing for birth control.

■ Hey, I don't mind you heckling me, but people are trying to sleep.

■ Hecklers are a lot like snow – no two flakes are exactly alike.

■ I have no problem with you speaking your mind, providing you have first used it to think.

■ I refuse to have a battle of wits with an unarmed person.

■ I thought alcoholics were supposed to be anonymous.

■ I'm happy to know your voice works. Too bad it isn't connected to anything.

■ I'm surprised to see you here. I didn't even know the circus was in town.

■ I've always wondered what became of that kid who played the banjo in *Deliverance*.

■ Is there a type of life form out there that we don't know about?

■ One more outburst like that and you'll never deliver

pizza in this town again.

- Pretend you're a Lithuanian and secede from the audience.
- Sir, have you ever considered changing your mind – for one with a larger capacity.
- Sir, please hold your comments until after everyone has left the auditorium, including me.
- Sir, they say that a word to the wise is sufficient. But in this case, I'd better repeat what I said.
- Talker on plane. Ask how much he paid for his ticket. Tell him you paid half that and got a coupon for two free drinks.
- Thank you for giving us a piece of your mind, but you should have left something for yourself.
- Thank you for heckling. It lets me know someone is still awake.
- There are times when we should all feel free to exercise our rights – especially the right to remain silent.
- There is no evidence that the tongue is connected to the brain.
- When I was a young man... That is when you first started to ask your questions...
- Why don't you exercise your right to remain silent?
- You don't get out much do you?
- You make a lot of sense for an incoherent person.
- Your voice sounds cultivated but you are using too much fertilizer.
- I wonder what language truck drivers are using, now that everyone is using theirs.

Holiday

■ Christmas card from mortgage holder: "... from our house to our house."

■ Christmas gifts - family crest stamper for ravioli...radio in a wig...chocolate chess set ...video tombstone...splattered windshield bug chart...water mattress with live sea animals ...VP Gore portrait

Stop believing in Santa Claus and you get underwear.

handpainted on black velvet... Bill Clinton copper portrait mold for gelatin...fake fish for water cooler.

- Christmas is the time for passing out gifts. New Year's Day is the time for passing out.

- Christmas is when you get the impression that God created the world in six days and the seventh day created batteries to make it all work.

- Christmas shopping: When a store can have 245 sales clerks – and all of them on break.

- Even when the boss says, "Merry Christmas," it sounds like an order.

- Halloween is when kids try to scare you. I believe in scaring them right back. When they ring your doorbell — offer them a job.

- I gave my wife a Christmas present that left her speechless. It was three weeks before she'd talk to me again.

- I had to convince my kids that I was Santa Claus and my wife that I wasn't.

- I think it's great to be home for the holidays. I only wish my in-laws felt the same way.

- I'm not going to celebrate New Year's Eve in a room filled with balloons, noisemakers and people wearing funny hats. I had enough of that during the campaign.

- Mothers never let you grow up. Mine still tells my age in months.

- My neighbor got into trouble for doing his Christmas shopping early – three hours before the store opened.

- Never try to guess your wife's size. Just buy her anything marked "PETITE" and hold on to the sales receipt.
- New Year's eve is when you go in like a lion and go out like a light.
- New Year's eve is when you're better off if your car won't start.
- On July 4, 1776, King George III of England noted in his diary: "Nothing of importance happened today."
- Parents Prayer: "May this be the Christmas when Barbie goes out, gets herself a job and buys her own clothes.
- Santa is that jolly old gent who goes "Ho! Ho! Ho!" And you'd laugh too if you had to work only one day a year.
- Show me a kid who doesn't believe in Santa and I'll show you a rebel without a Claus.
- The Christmas presents of today are the garage sales of tomorrow.
- The Post Office helped me celebrate Mother's Day by delivering the Christmas card I sent her last year.
- There's a very good reason why Santa Claus is so jolly. He knows it will be a whole year before he has to get near kids again.
- When you ask kids if they believe in Santa Claus, you have to judge their answer from three different perspectives: The level of their maturity; the level of their sophistication; and the level of their greed.

■ You know you've hit middle age when you don't need a pillow to play Santa Claus.

Insults

If I promise to miss you, will you go away?

■ (City) isn't the end of the world... but you can see it from here!

■ A gifted student. Any grade higher than a C was a gift.

■ A man of vision, of insight, of foresight. A man who once said to Oliver North, "Who's gonna know."

■ A man who has never approved of sexual license – mostly because he has never been able to get a learner's permit.

■ According to Census, New Jersey has the densest population. They also have the most people per square mile.

■ Consider a nose job. Of course, in your case, they'll have to start with your feet.

■ Could I borrow your IQ? I'm going out with an idiot tonight.

■ Did you ever hear of a kid playing "accountant" – even if he wanted to be one?

■ Don't get carried away about the men who wrote the Constitution. What else is there to do during the summer in Philadelphia.

■ Don't move. I want to forget you just the way you are.

■ Eat! He's the only guy I know that uses a battery-operated fork.

■ Eat! We're talking about a man who can overcome, outwit and outmaneuver any diet.

■ Ever have one of those days when you felt depressed, downcast and miserable and you weren't in Cleveland?

■ Ever notice how when somebody makes a poo-poo in the elevator, everybody always turns and looks at you.

■ Everytime he opens his mouth, his foot falls out.

■ For years people have said he would never amount to much. These are people who never saw him step on a scale.

■ George Jessel about Al Jolson: "His funeral was well attended by those who wanted to make sure."

■ Give him a penny for his thoughts and you'll have change coming.

■ He can do something that most lower animals can't do like standing in front of a crowd and put both feet in his mouth.

■ He can stay longer in an hour than most people do in a week.

■ He couldn't be with us tonight. He's at the doctors having something removed from his hand — an ingrown bottle.

■ He does 100-yard sprints in a 90-yard gym.

■ He has a slightly distracted look about him — like he's trying to remember his Social Security number.

■ He has found a direction in life. Too bad, it's toward

the refrigerator.

■ He has given new meaning to the term "casual sex." All of his partners yawn a lot.

■ He has no respect for age unless it's bottled.

■ He holds the record for the 100-yard stagger.

■ He puts his foot in his mouth so often, he's developed athlete's throat

■ He saw *Guess Who's Coming to Dinner* twice and missed the answer twice.

■ He switched to scotch without giving up bourbon.

■ He was a lookout for Pearl Harbor.

■ He was an amazing child. When other kids were just learning to say individual words, he was already boring them with complete sentences.

■ He wouldn't be where he is today if he hadn't started at the bottom and stayed there.

■ He's a great admirer of his wife's husband.

■ He's been an exhibitionist for 25 years – and what does he have to show for it?

■ He's been to the School of Hard Knocks. Too bad they were to his head.

■ He's down on everything he's not up on.

■ He's like a eunuch in a harem: He's there every night, he watches it happen, he sees how it's done, but he just can't do it himself.

■ He's like a stopped clock – right about twice a day and wrong the rest of the time.

■ He's never been concerned about baldness because he believes that bald-headed men are sexy – and he

discovered they are but only to bald-headed women.
- He's never been drunk in his life – at his own expense.
- He's not too bright. He took an Ignorance Equivalency Test.
- He's the low life of the party.
- Her hardest decision is when to start middle age.
- His favorite drink is his next one.
- His three favorite forms of entertainment are movies, TV and mirrors.
- I am not conceited, though I do have every reason to be.
- I can remember when he weighed 165 lbs. He was a cute baby.
- I enjoyed talking to you. My mind needed a rest.
- I have the world's laziest postman. If it's raining or snowing, he stays home and reads me my mail.
- I knew a girl who was possessed – by almost everybody.
- I like the way he babbles over with enthusiasm.
- I said good morning and he was stuck for an answer.
- I understand you were arrested for indecent exposure and the only thing showing was your face.
- I wanted to get dressed up in something weird and far out tonight and make everybody laugh – but I see you beat me to it.
- I wasn't swearing, I was just quoting _____.
- I'd put a curse on you, but somebody beat me to it.
- If brains were dynamite, you couldn't blow your nose.

■ If he fell into a vat of whiskey, he'd raise its alcohol content.

■ If he were to make a film of the highlights of his life, there wouldn't be enough footage to choose from.

■ If he's God's gift to women, God must shop at K-Mart

■ If Moses had known you, there would have been one more commandment.

■ If you have your life to live over again, do it overseas.

■ If you were to list the 10 smartest (dumbest) people, who would be the other nine?

■ If your I.Q. ever reaches as high as your age, it'll surprise the medical world.

■ Investment banking has become to productive enterprise in this country, what mud wrestling is to the performing arts.

■ Is your family happy? Or do you go home at night?

■ It makes as much sense as a eunuch taking Vitamin E.

■ It makes as much sense as buying a car with a sunroof in Seattle.

■ "Lend me a quarter. I want to call a friend." "Here's 50 cents. Call both of them."

■ Like talking to a fifth of (_____).

■ Looking at you, I get a tremendous desire to be lonesome.

■ Man in Atlantic City demanded a room facing the ocean, and was given a room facing the ocean — the Pacific Ocean!

■ Makes you feel warm all over. So can the 24-hour flu.

- May we have the pleasure of your absence.
- My uncle performed a community service several years ago — he moved out of the community.
- No tact. He'd invite a mermaid to a fish fry.
- Not a compulsive gambler... a compulsive loser.
- Not saying he's a jerk but he'll do until one comes along.
- Not very upscale. If he had been Adam in the Garden of Eden, his fig leaf would have been polyester.
- She reminds me of Jeannie with the light brown teeth.
- She was chosen Miss America at 21. There were few Americans in those days.
- She's more than words can describe. Although I've got a few that come mighty close.
- So vain that he won't share a mirror with his own image.
- Some people bring happiness wherever they go. You bring it whenever you go.
- Sometimes it's hard to believe there were only two jackasses aboard Noah's ark.
- Spell Mississippi. State or river?
- Talkative. If she ever ate her words, she'd put on 50 pounds.
- That's a nice suit. But what will you do if your horse gets cold?
- That's a rather broad statement for such a narrow mind.
- The last time I saw him he was walking down Lover's Lane holding his own hand. – *Fred Allen*

- There is no evidence that the tongue is connected to the brain.
- There's always room for one bore.
- Two things I don't like about you — your face.
- Vain — if he were a rooster, he would believe that the sun rose just to hear him crow.
- When he leaves the room, it's like a breath of fresh air.
- When he tries to collect his thoughts, all he needs is a thimble.
- When his wife looks at him, she gets a tremendous desire to be lonesome.
- Why don't you go to a dentist and have some wisdom teeth put in.
- Why that face when his best friend is a plastic surgeon?
- With the right coaching, you could be a nobody.
- Women who most resent being considered sex objects, usually aren't.
- Writer to photographer: you must have a good camera. Photographer to writer: You must have a good typewriter.
- You don't have paranoia. Everybody does hate you.
- You're an example of what happens when you wear a beanie with the propeller on the inside.
- You've got to be taught to hate. Thank you for teaching me so much.

Introductions

- May 18, 1980 – anniversary of eruption of Mt. St. Helen's). If there's one human being who could blow that much smoke and hot air, its our speaker tonight..."
- A closed mouth gathers no feet.
- A fearless man. The only time he's ever thrown in the

He dresses like an unmade bed.

towel is when he's checking out of a hotel.

■ A man of few words but he keeps them very busy.

■ A man who has brought new prominence to this field. I would not be wrong saying he has done for (_____) what Dr. Ruth has done for heavy breathing, or, (the Boston strangler for door-to-door salesmen.)

■ After that introduction, you may not recognize me. I usually wear a much smaller head.

■ It's all right to have a big house but who has a walk-in mailbox?

■ America is still the land of opportunity especially if you happen to be a businessman in Japan.

■ An astute businessman, his latest success is a summer camp for overweight kids. The kids don't lose any weight. He just sends them home in bigger clothes.

■ And now, ladies and gentlemen, here he is — your friend...and his.

■ Barbara Bush and photographers: "Don't disturb her during her talk." "Shoot her before she talks."

■ Can't be here tonight because he has a multiple concussion. He was struck by a thought.

■ Chairman recognizes committee, waiters, etc. Then said to me: "You don't mind if I don't introduce you just yet, do you?" I said no. She said: "Great, because they're having such a wonderful time out there I hate to ruin it."

■ Cheap: Who else has a windup pacemaker?

■ Conceited: He could gain 5 pounds just from swallowing his pride.

■ Conceited: His idea of being unfaithful is turning away from the mirror.

■ Conservative? If he had been Adam in the Garden of Eden, he would have had a button-down fig leaf.

■ Does Imelda Marcos know her shoe size?

■ Drinks to forget; last night forgot to stand up.

■ Each of these boys is a soloist. If you don't believe me, listen to them when they try to play together.

■ Every day in America...100,000 move to another home and 18,000 to another state...40 Americans turn 100, about 5,800 become 65 and 8,000 become 40...167 businesses go bankrupt and 689 new ones start up...105 Americans become millionaires...Americans buy 45,000 new cars and trucks and smash up 87,000...20,000 write letters to the President...6,300 get divorced and 13,000 get married...Dogs bite 11,000 people including 20 mail carriers.. we eat 75 acres of pizza, 53 million hot dogs, 167 million eggs, 3 million gallons of ice cream and 3,000 tons of candy. — *Reader's Digest*

■ Grew up in tough neighborhood. Obituaries were written two weeks in advance.

■ Grew up in tough neighborhood, also strong. Where else can you see people jogging with a car radio under each arm?

■ He can follow you through a revolving door and come out first.

■ He claims he is a self-made man. At least he's not blaming God.

- He could be described as charming, intelligent and entertaining, and one day he will be.
- He doesn't have an enemy in the world. He's outlived them all.
- He doesn't know art but he also doesn't know what he likes.
- He has been called loquacious – a man who is in love with language; who never uses one word when ten will do. Rumor has it that when he prays, a deep majestic voice from above can be heard saying: Look, I don't have all day!
- He is the kind of person who believes that if he'd never been born, God would have a lot of explaining to do. – *Milton Berle*
- He makes mistakes and will be the second to admit it
- He never qualfied for the book *Who's Who,* but he is listed in *Who's That?*
- He puts his foot in his mouth so often, his favorite flavor is toe.
- He rarely accepts speaking engagements. After you hear his presentation, you'll understand why.
- He won't take no for an answer. When he arrives at the Pearly Gates, Saint Peter probably will have to call security.
- He was going to write a book...but found he could buy them for $4.95.
- He's one of the greatest in the country. In the city, not so good.
- He's so optimistic, he'd buy a burial suit with two

pairs of pants.

■ He's such a procrastinator that he subscribes to *USA TOMORROW.*

■ He's the father of a 7-pound baby boy. Wait until his wife hears about it.

■ His idea of diplomacy is letting someone else have his way.

■ His idea of pumping iron is lifting a knife, fork and spoon.

■ His record is one out of two — and that's just applying his spray deodorant.

■ However sketchy my introduction may have been...

■ I can promise you that our next speaker will not bore you until he opens his mouth.

■ He knows what it is to be hungry, but he always went right to a restaurant.

■ I know you believe you understand what you think I said but I am not sure you realize that what you heard is not what I meant.

■ I think we owe a great debt of gratitude to our chainnan, who has so capably chaired this organization...The Irish believe that a leprechaun kisses every baby that is born. If the kiss is on the brow, the child is destined to become an intellectual. If the kiss is on the eyes, the child will become a great beauty; if on the fingers, a great artist. I'm not in a position to tell you where the leprechaun kissed Mr. Jones, but you will have to admit he makes a wonderful chairman.

- I would like to introduce a man who's going places. Unfortunately, he stopped here first.
- If he had lived in ancient days, Rome *would* have been built in a day.
- If the Alamo had a back door, Texas would own Mexico.
- If you can't say something nice about someone, you shouldn't say anything at all. Let me present...
- If you want me to talk for 10 minutes, I'll come next week. If you want me to talk for an hour, I'll come tonight.
- Imelda Marcos. Big shoes to fill.
- It gives me great pleasure to introduce our next guest. Obviously it doesn't take much to give me great pleasure.
- It's about as exciting as watching a nudist sliding down a banister.
- Just because he's paranoid doesn't mean someone isn't after him!
- Looks like he just finished seeing 200 slides of his neighbor's vacation in Cleveland.
- Looks like the one who asks for ketchup in a French restaurant.
- Mark Twain used to introduce himself because of so many bad introductions, such as the man who said: I don't know anything about this man except for two things. One is that he has never been in jail. And the other, I don't know why.
- John Wayne said: "Talk low; talk slow and don't say

too much."

- The next guest has had considerable experience speaking to large, attentive audiences. He makes obscene phone calls on party lines.
- Next we have a mystery speaker. I have no idea what he's doing here.
- Not an easy time for him. His inflatable doll ran away with the Goodyear blimp.
- Not two-faced. If so, why would he wear the one he has.
- Nothing but an innocent grandstander.
- On his last birthday, he sent his parents a telegram of congratulations.
- Our next guest is one of a kind – which is plenty.
- Our next guest will test how strongly you believe in free speech.
- Our next scheduled speaker had a reputation for intellectual and indepth speeches – so we replaced him.
- Our next speaker and I go back a long way — He's been my most intelligent, generous and honest friend for as long as I've been a liar.
- Our speaker is a free thinker. Unfortunately, he isn't a free speaker.
- Our next speaker is known by those who have heard of him.
- Our next speaker needs no introduction — I'm just killing time until he's ready.
- Our next speaker never lacked for self-confidence. Every Christmas when he hears someone mention

the Three Wise Men, he wonders who the other two are.

■ Please hold your applause until the next speaker is finished, and I come out again.

■ So old, he can remember when Ronald Reagan could.

■ Some of you may recognize our next guest, especially those who watch *America's Most Wanted.*

■ The last time he gave a speech, the audience kept yelling: "Up in front!"

■ They say there is a time and place for everything. Unfortunately, now is the time and place for our next speaker.

■ They say you can't have too much of a good thing, but tonight we're going to try.

■ Two cities claim the birth of our distinguished speaker — Chicago and Detroit. Chicago claims he was born in Detroit and Detroit claims he was born in Chicago.

■ Two kinds of speakers I can do without — those who never stop to think and those who never think to stop.

■ Upset. Went to the bar and remembered to bring money

■ We had planned to have entertainment this evening, but we invited our next guest, instead.

■ When things looked bad in the Korean War, he volunteered to go to the states for help.

■ While driving over here, I concentrated very hard on how to introduce our next speaker. I concentrated so hard, I'd like to introduce the person responsible for my smashed fender.

■ Wouldn't call him a liar. Just say he lives on the other side of the facts.

■ You all should be pleased this man is with us tonight. Otherwise, he might be at your house.

■ You have to be impressed by this man. It's the first time I've ever seen a polyester power tie.

Jobs

■ A job takes you no where; a career will take you any-
where you want to go.
■ Half of all Americans are afraid of losing their jobs.
The other half already lost them.
■ I began to sense I had problems at work when I re-
turned from lunch and found pictures of somebody

I once had a job as a memory specialist.
I can't recall why they fired me.

83

else's kids on my desk.

■ I once had a job going door-to-door selling "No solicitor" signs.

■ I quit my job repairing pencil sharpeners because it seemed pointless.

■ I went for a job interview. I told the guy I wasn't looking for *work*. All I wanted was a *job*.

■ I'm really upset. Last week I had to use up a sick day from work because I was sick.

■ I've got an employee working for me who does so little, she never knows when she's finished.

■ If the Maytag Repairman really wants something to do, he should work for NASA.

■ It might be true that hard work never hurt anyone, but why take a chance?

■ Millions of Americans aren't working – but thank God they've got jobs.

■ Our goal should be just out of reach but not out of sight.

■ People may forget how fast you did a job, but they will remember how well you did it.

■ Personal interviewer said to job applicant, "I see you have been careful not to become over-qualified.

■ Sign in factory: Firings will continue until morale improves.

■ The best time to look for work is after you get the job.

■ The country's biggest problem is the large number of unemployed still on the payroll.

■ The Egyptian pyramids took 420 years to complete. They must have used the same contractor we're using.

■ Too many people are so busy being good that they don't have time to be excellent.

■ We must view young people not as empty bottles to be filled, but as candles to be lit.

■ When I applied for this job, I was told my salary would be based on my skills, training and experience. There's always a catch.

■ When it comes to its employees, our company is very compassionate. You get a day off to attend a funeral, and a whole week off it it's yours.

After six months of computer dating,
I'm ready to go back to women.

Jokes

■ A doctor said the best thing to do is give up drinking and smoking, get up early and go to bed early. The patient said no, and asked: "What's second best?"

■ "I understand you're not going to Rome this summer." "That was last year. This year we're not going to London."

■ Those trousers don't make you look fat. ("You are fat.")

■ Please be gentle. It's my first time. ("This week!")

■ An 83-year old man took Vitamin E to get his wife pregnant. She went to the doctor who said she was. She called husband and said, "You devil, I'm pregnant." He asked, "Who's calling?"

■ There was a big fire in a small midwestern town. The heat was intense and spreading. Owner called the local fire department, who came but said the fire was too much for them. The owner called around offering $10,000 to put it out. One fire company agreed and the fire truck came. The truck drove straight into the heart of the fire and put it out. When the owner paid the driver, he asked, "What will you do with the money?" "Get the brakes fixed on that damn fire truck," he said.

■ A boxer was being pounded in a fight. His manager kept telling him, "You're doing great, kid. He ain't laid a glove on ya." At end of 9th round, the bloodied and bruised boxer winced when his manager said he hadn't been hit yet. He told his manager to keep his eye on the referee, "Because someone is beating the Hell out of me."

■ A carpet-layer surveyed a newly installed carpet. He reached in his shirt pocket for pack of cigarettes. They were missing. He noticed at same time a lump under the carpet in middle of room — about the size of a pack of cigarettes. Not wanting to take carpet up, he hammered the lump flat. Then discovered his pack of cigarettes. He lit one up as the homeowner came out of the house and asked: "Hey, have you seen my son's gerbil?"

■ A collection agency sent a letter to a man saying: "We are surprised that we have not received anything from you." A letter came back: "No reason to be surprised. I didn't send anything."

■ A cucumber is a terrible thing to waste.

■ A driver of a small sedan braked hastily as a Porsche came hurtling around a sharp bend in a narrow road. The Porsche driver yelled out, "Pig." The driver of the small car shouted back, "Cow." The he drove around the bend himself — and crashed head on into the biggest pig he had ever seen.

■ A man telling a friend about unintentionally driving through a puddle and splashing a pedestrian, a visitor from Florida. Friend asked how he knew he was from Florida. "Because I could hear him yelling something about the sun and the beach."

■ A touring opera company has advertised for local volunteers to serve as spear carriers. This is known as free lancing.

■ About as silly as leaving the porch light on for Jimmy Hoffa.

■ Adam was stupid. Had a choice between the world's only woman and an apple – and took the apple.

■ Advertising brings quick results. Yesterday we advertised for a security guard, and last night we were robbed.

■ An airline baggage man found a dog in one of their carriers was dead. He frantically sent someone out to buy a similar dog. Imagine the owners surprise at finding the dog alive. She was transporting him to be buried.

■ An antelope and a lion entered a diner and sat in a booth near the window. When the waiter came over, the antelope said: "I'll take a bowl of hay and a side order of radishes." The waiter said: "And what will your friend be having?" The antelope replied: "Nothing." The waiter asked: "Why not? Isn't he hungry?" The antelope shook his head in disbelief and said: "Hey, if he was hungry, would I be sitting here?"

■ Ant and elephant made love. The elephant died. The ant said: "One night of passion and I will spend the rest of my life digging a grave."

■ Aunt: "You don't like my gift? I asked you if you liked large or small checks." Nephew: "But I didn't think you meant neckties."

■ Bar owner called at 3 a.m. by drunk who asked what time he opened. "I wouldn't let someone in your condition in." Caller said: "I don't want to get in; I want to get out."

■ A band was contracted to play from 8:30 p.m. until 1:30 a.m. At 10 p.m., all but one person had left The band kept playing until 11:30 p.m. The band leader asked if the man wanted anything special played for him. The man said: "I'm a janitor and I don't want to stay — all I want is to go home."

■ A restaurant in Mexico had Bull Balls on the menu. A visitor ordered them and raved about them. When he returned to restaurant a year later, he ordered the same thing. This time the balls were smaller. The waiter explained: "The bull does not always lose."

■ Bum asked for work, and was told to paint the porch green. The painter said: "I did it, but that was not a

Porsche. It was a Mercedes."

■ Burglar stuck gun in man's back. Man spun around and flung him across the alley, karate chops battered the man's face, dislocated his jaw, broke his ribs and arm. The battered burglar cried out: "Ain't you ever gonna call a cop?"

■ Calvin Coolidge was having a dinner at the White House. His guests watched closely. The President poured coffee and cream into a saucer. Others followed. Then he put the saucer on the floor for his cat.

■ Can't applaud with one hand.

■ Columbus set sail on August 3, 1492, for the Orient. He ended up in America. In the process setting a pattern that hasn't changed in 500 years, men still refuse to ask for directions.

■ Contractor offered money to a builder to hold up the contract. Builder said "no" and would not accept money. It would be dishonest. The contractor said then, he would give the builder a Cadillac. Then the builder said he would take two.

■ Custer hired two men to serve as scouts and offered them a dollar for each Sioux tribesman they captured or killed. They camped for the night near the Little Bighorn River. At dawn, one of them was awakened by a sharp prod and looked up. Standing over him was a fierce Sioux tribesman and behind him were hundreds more. He nudged the other scout and said excitedly: "Wake up. We're rich!"

■ Did you read President Ford's *Humor and the Presidency?* Yes, and I fell off the chair laughing.

■ Difference between caucus and cactus. Cactus has pricks on the outside.

■ Driver got a picture in the mail from State Police that had his license plate, a recorded speed, the date and the speeding fee. The driver sent back the ticket with a photo of a $100 bill for the fine.

■ A driverless car was rolling. A woman jumped in and pulled emergency brake. "I stopped the car." Man said: "I know. I was pushing it."

■ A man drove through the red lights. When questioned why, he said, "My cousin does it." Then he stopped at green light. Why? "My cousin might be out driving."

■ During prohibition, I was forced to live for days on nothing but food and water. — *W.C. Fields*

■ An elderly man found a bottle, complete with Genie. The Genie agreed to grant him one wish. The man said he'd had a fight with his brother 30 years ago and wished his brother would forgive him. The Genie said, "Most men would have wished for wealth or fame – is it because you are old and dying? "No way, but my brother is, and he's worth $60 million!"

■ Famous British conductor remembered music but not names. At a cocktail party, he saw a woman he knew but couldn't remember her name, but recalled she had a sister. "What's your sister doing now," he asked. "She's still the queen."

Invested $10,000 on a prized dog for breeding purposes but found out he barked with a lisp.

■ Farmer and wife. The farmer opened his trunk. Inside were three ears of corn, and $10,000. His wife asked what it was for. Farmer said he was unfaithful, and he threw an ear of corn in the trunk each time. Wife asked about the money. Farmer said every time he got a bushel, he sold it.

■ Four friends were hunting bear. Three had guns and Norm had a hunting knife. He said he could catch a bear with his bare hands. He left his three friends in the cabin and went out to find bear. His friends heard a cry from Norm to open the door. A bear was right behind him. They opened the door, Norm jumped to one side and the bear ran into the cabin. Norm called out, "Okay, skin that one, I'll get another."

■ Got into trouble by smuggling books into(_____). (Your state.)

■ An old man, known for his stinginess, was dying. He called his grandson to his bedside. The boy expectantly leaned close to hear what his grandfather would say. The old man reached under his pillow and holding out his hand said, "Do you want to buy a gold watch?"

■ Grandmother on beach with young grandson. A wave swept him out to sea. Grandmother pleaded to God to save him. Another wave swept him safely back to the beach. Grandmother looked to the heavens and cried out: "He had a hat."

■ Greeting cards: sorry I missed your coronation…congratulations on your presidential pardon… hurrah for your new hamster…so now you're a cardinal…thank you for the assorted mushrooms…good luck on your release from the witness-protection program.

■ Have you ever read *Love Story?* No, and I have to say I'm sorry.

■ Have you read all of Dante's *Divine Comedy?* Hell, no.

■ Have you read the new Yuppie classic, *Uncle Tom's Condo?*

■ I don't know what makes the boss tick, but I sure know what makes him explode.

■ I know why gas station bathrooms are always locked. It's to keep someone from wandering in and cleaning one.

■ I shot an arrow into the air. It fell to earth. I knew not where. Dial 911 . I'll try to work his hat off.

■ I used to think I was indecisive but now I'm not so sure.

■ I went on a diet, swore off drinking and heavy eating and in 14 days I lost two weeks. — *Joe E. Lewis*

■ If you think before you speak, the other guy gets his joke in first.

■ Indian to Pilgrim: "Now do I understand; you want to have a picnic outside in late November?"

■ It wasn't the airplanes. It was beauty killed the beast. Falling off the Empire State Building didn't do him any good, either.

■ It's deja vu all over again. — *Yogi Berra.*

■ It's easy to grin when your ship comes in; and you've got the stock market beat. But the man worth while is the man who can smile, when his shorts are too tight in the seat.

■ Jesse James and his band of outlaws stopped a train, unloaded all of the passengers and separated men from women. Man stepped forward and said: "Jesse James, you can have our money, you can have our jewels, but you cannot take the honor of our women." An elderly woman stepped forward and said: "Don't you tell Jesse James how to rob a train."

■ Knight returned to castle in total disarray and wounded. "What hath befallen you, Sir Knight?" "Sire, I have been laboring in your service, robbing and pillaging your enemies to the west." The Lord said: "I have no enemies to the west." The knight said: "You do now."

■ Man applied for a job as a prison guard. Warden asked if he could handle the tough guys. "No problem. If they don't behave, out they go."

■ Man who ate dog food, was killed chasing a car.

■ Man called room service and ordered two boiled eggs, one runny and the other like rubber; grilled bacon left on the plate to get cold; burnt toast that crumbles; hard frozen butter, a lukewarm weak pot of coffee. Waiter said that would be difficult to produce. The man said: "You didn't find it difficult yesterday."

■ A couple found a man who had fallen outside a bar. They helped him stand up, but he fell again. They figured he was drunk and they should take him home. Despite his protests, they got his address from his wallet and took him to his house. The wife answered the door. She seemed surprised, but thanked them and asked, "Where's his wheelchair?"

■ Man in cab forgot his wallet. Asked driver to stop at hardware store so he could buy a flashlight to look for $100 bill he dropped in cab. When he came out, the cab was gone.

■ A man in jail sent his son a letter telling him that he had buried the stolen money in his field. The sheriff screening the mail had the field plowed and soil turned over thoroughly but found nothing. Son asked his father what he should do now? "Plant the potatoes," his father said.

■ Man of feeling and compassion, was concerned for all living creatures. He broke down and cried when his girlfriend told him the rabbit died.

■ Man running from train, train bumps him. Spectator asked why didn't he run off the tracks and up an incline. "If I couldn't beat him on the flat, what would I do on the side of the hill."

■ A man won the lottery. Went to a stockbroker's office and said he wanted to open a ★#%!#★ account. He was ordered out. Manager asked what the problem was. "I won $12 million and want to open a ★#%!#★ account." Manager asked, "Are these ★#%!#★ people bothering you?"

■ Mirror over my bed broke. Now I'll have seven years

of bad sex.

■ My dog is very patriotic. He chases only American cars.

■ NASA had the best astronauts from America, Russia and Japan to participate in joint two-year mission in space. Told they could bring anything that didn't weigh more than 125 pounds. American took a wife. Japanese, a collection of Greek books. Russian, cigars. At the end, American stepped out with twin boys. The Japanese spoke perfect Greek. Russian said: "All right. Anybody got a match?"

■ Near-missing slogans...Preparation G...When you care enough to spend $1.25...Sam Cassidy and the Sundance Kid...Los Angeles Law...Swiss Army fork...People who live in glass houses shouldn't throw up...Danny's inferno...Nice tries finish last...The rest is yet to come.

■ A king said he would give his daughter in marriage to any man brave enough to swim a lake filled with piranha. The suitors all held back until one dove in, swam like mad and made it to the other side. He immediately started running back toward to the other side. The king said, "Are you hurrying to find my daughter?" The man said, "No, I'm after the guy who pushed me."

99

■ Two hunters returned to their favorite lake to hunt moose. They chartered a sea plane to get there. The pilot was afraid the lake was too short to take off and land, but the hunters told him, "We did it last year." The pilot said he would return for them in three days. When he returned, he saw the two hunters, their gear and three moose. The pilot was sure the lake was too short to take off with three moose. The hunters said, "We did it last year." "Well, if one bush pilot could do it, so can I." They lifted from the water, climbing to clear a stand of trees – and almost made it! When they came to, one of them asked where they were! "About 30 yards further than last year."

■ Not a great looker. When I wanted to get romantic, the first thing I took off was my glasses.

■ Nun/Bedpan. Three nuns were traveling and ran out of gas. They needed to walk to a gas station, but the only thing they could find to fill with gas was a bed pan. Came back and the three were pouring the gas into the tank from the bedpan. A passing truck driver noticed the activity, and said: "I wish I had your faith, Sisters."

■ Parachute. A skydiver falling but the chute failed to open. He was surprised to see a man coming up toward him. He asked: "What do you know about parachutes?" The other flyer asked: "What do you know about gas stoves?"

■ A man bought a parrot guaranteed to have a large vocabulary. A few days later he went back to the pet store to complain that the parrot was not talking. "That's strange, he usually climbs his little ladder...""Ladder? Can I buy one?" Two days later, the parrot still wasn't talking. Store owner said, "Strange, he always climbed his little ladder, looked in his little mirror..." "Mirror, can I buy one?" Over the next week he bought a swing and a bell. He returned to tell the pet shop owner that the bird had died. "Did he say anything?" "Yes, he said, 'Didn't they sell birdseed?'"

■ Parrot/Burglar. Parrot said "Jesus will not like this." Burglar said: "Shut up!" Parrot: "Sic him, Jesus." And a big dog went at the burglar.

■ People are impressed by the size of my new office. Actually, I'm still in my old office but I bought smaller furniture.

■ Photog hired plane for aerial photos of forest fire. Rushed to airport and hopped in idling plane. "Take off!" He asked the pilot to make some low level passes. Pilot asked why? "Because I'm a photographer." "You mean you're not the instructor?"

■ Police stopped driver for going through stop sign. Driver said he slowed down. Cop beat on his head: "Do you want me to stop or slow down?"

■ Professor and farmer on train were bored and decided to try some riddles. Professor agreed he would give farmer a dollar for each riddle he did not know and farmer would give the professor 50 cents. Farmer asked, "What has three legs walking and two legs flying." Professor did not know and gave farmer a dollar. Farmer also didn't know and gave professor 50 cents.

■ A man was in a psychiatrist's office for testing. The doctor drew a circle on a piece of paper. The man said it reminded him of sex. The doctor then drew a triangle. The man said it reminded him of sex. The doctor then drew a square – same answer. The doctor said, "You're depraved." Man said, "Me! You're the one drawing the dirty pictures."

■ Psychiatrists. Most difficult case. Man believed a rich uncle in South America was going to leave him a fortune. Waited all day for a make believe letter to arrive from a fictitious attorney. He just sat and waited. Took eight years to cure him. And then that stupid letter arrived..." - *Milton Berle*

■ Sam Goldwyn's malaprops and mixed metaphors: a verbal contract isn't worth the paper it's printed on...

every Tom, Dick and Harry is named William... for your information, I would like to ask a question... include me out... don't talk to me while I'm interrupting.

■ Saved my life during WW II. Hid me in cellar on (local street).

■ Two boys were fighting over who would play Joseph in the school play. One was disappointed but agreed to play the innkeeper. When Joseph and Mary arrived at the inn, the innkeeper said, "Come in." Joseph said, "I'm not taking my wife into a place like this."

■ Smith's clothing store was not doing much business. On the way home, Smith met Jones who said: "Smith I'm terribly sorry to hear about the fire in your store yesterday." Smith whispered, "For heaven's sake, not yesterday – tomorrow!"

■ So I said to the Godfather: "Sticks and stones might break my bones but names will never harm me. And I was right. He sent over Mickey Sticks and Louis Stones and they broke my bones."

■ Stewardess: "I'd rather commit adultery than drink scotch." Flyer: "I didn't know we had a choice."

103

■ The airline lost my luggage. I'm used to that, but the guy at the baggage claim was wearing my clothes.

■ "This is the captain speaking. We are experiencing a little mild turbulence." ("Our Father...").

■ Truck driver at diner was harassed by three bikers. He left and one biker said to waitress: "He's not much of a man." She said: "He's not much of a driver either. He just backed his truck over three motorcycles."

■ Trust. A man who was going to be away from home for two months asked a friend to look after things, mostly his wife. Two hours later, his friend called and said: "You gave me the wrong key."

■ Two drunks in a bar. One passed out and fell flat on his face. The other said: "That's what I like about Sam. He knows when to quit."

■ Two friends walking on the beach run under a dock for cover during a thunderstorm. The dock collapses, injuring them slightly. They are victims of pier pressure.

■ Two ladies in cemetery. Here lies John Smith, a politician and an honest man. "They had to stick two people in one grave," one asked.

■ Two men died and waited at the Pearly Gates for admission. St. Peter said there is room for only one and asked: "Which one of you is more humble."

■ Two men in woods run across a bear. One puts on his running shoes. Other man said "you don't think that running shoes will help you outrun the bear." Other man: "I don't have to outrun the bear. I only have to outrun you."

■ Two parrots: One swearing and rowdy, the other — owned by minister — prayed all day. They got together and bad parrot asked other parrot for loving. Minister's parrot said: "That's what I've been praying for."

■ Ugly child. A mother overhead someone saying her child was ugly. She was upset and crying. A lady passing by tried to comfort her. She told her to brush it off and said: "Here's a banana for your monkey."

■ A neighbor asked about the vase on the mantle. The lady said it contained her husband's ashes. He wasn't dead – just too lazy to look for an ashtray.

■ Warden asked the condemned man what he wanted for his last meal. Man: "I'll have mushrooms." Warden: "Why?" Man: "Always been afraid to eat them."

■ What do you mean I'm *fired?* I always thought slaves were *sold.*

■ What's the difference between a bad joke and a good joke? A bad joke begins with "What's the difference..."

■ When does life begin? Conception? Birth? No, when the kids leave the house and the dog dies.

■ When Hank Greensburg was general manager of the Cleveland Indians, one of his players returned his contract unsigned. Greensburg sent him a telegram: "In your haste to accept my terms, you forgot to sign the contract." The player returned: "In your haste to give me a raise, you put in the wrong figure."

■ Widow on farm. Two salesmen had a damaged car and a widow let them sleep overnight. Some years later, the widow died and left the farm to one of the salesmen. He was very surprised. The other salesman was shocked because he'd had a warm relationship with the widow but used his partner's name.

■ Wife berated her husband in a restaurant. "Of all the despicable people on this earth, you are the vilest!" People were staring. Husband: "You were right, my dear. And what else did you say to him?"

Kids

■ You are no longer a teenager when you become afraid of teenagers.

■ A major illness is one that keeps you from work when the kids are out of school.

■ A sign in their rooms — checkout time is 18 years.

■ A straight line is the shortest distance between a 3-year-old and anything that breaks.

Letter from camp –
"Broke a leg. Don't worry, not mine!"

■ Adolescents go through a rough time. My daughter came home crying, "Everyone at school hates me because I'm so popular."

■ Amazing how a little soap and water can turn a complete stranger into your own child.

■ An inferiority complex is any teenager who feels his parents are smarter than he is.

■ An optimist is a father who will let his son take the new car on a date. A pessimist is one who won't. A cynic is one who did.

■ Anyone who thinks that money can't buy happiness, has never sent their kids to summer camp.

■ Arguing with teenagers is like trying to put out a lightbulb by blowing on it.

■ Before I got married, I had six theories about bringing up children. Now I have six children and no theories. — *John Wilmot*, Earl of Rochester, 17th Century English poet.

■ I believe there is nothing wrong with my kids that a maximum security day care center couldn't handle.

■ Boy or girl? Let it grow up and decide.

■ I had trouble finding myself because my parents were always telling me to get lost.

■ I know kids make a lot of mistakes. Then again, mistakes make a lot of kids.

■ I know why 13 is an unlucky number – that's when kids become teenagers.

■ I love my kids. Someone has to.

■ I want my children to have all the things I never could

afford. Then I want to move in with them.

■ I'm afraid I'm going to have another man-to-man talk with my teenage son. I've forgotten some of what he told me.

■ I've stopped worrying about what the kids will be when they grow up. I'm too busy trying to figure out what they are now.

■ If you can find a machine that can remove the snow from your driveway faster than an 18-year-old boy who needs the car for a date, buy it.

■ It is the malady of the age that the young are so busy teaching us that they have no time to learn.

■ It isn't what a teenager knows that worries his parents. Its how he found out. — *Ann Landers*

■ It seldom occurs to teenagers that someday they will know as little as their parents.

■ It's very discouraging when you pin your kid's gloves to his sleeve – and then he loses the coat.

■ Junket is a guided tour through a teenager's room.

■ Kids are smart. We bought a 5-year-old a complete set of Peter Rabbit books. She uses them to sit on to reach the keys of her computer.

■ By the age of 15, the average boy has outgrown 34 pairs of shoes, 53 shirts and two parents.

■ Child saying alphabet. I'm praying but can't think of the right words so I just say all the letters. God will put them together for me because he knows what I'm thinking.

■ Children always brighten up a home. They never turn

off the lights.
- Don't let anyone tell you you're too young to worry. It's never too early to start
- Duke of Windsor said the thing that impressed him most about America is the way parents obey their children.
- Ever have one of those days when you wish you had been born *after* your children?
- Father asked if he knew what Abraham Lincoln was doing "at your age." Son said he didn't know but he knew what he was doing at *your* age. He was president.
- For a peaceful Halloween, when the first group of kids knock on the door, give them a plate of liver and onions.
- For safety, the city has posted signs reading: "Watch out for children. They may be armed."
- Good to have someone around the house who understands computers.
- He is mean, quick-tempered, destructive and uncommunicative. This doesn't bother me because — I have kids of my own.
- How come I can remember when Shirley Temple was a kid, but I can't remember when I was a kid?
- I can't understand it. I taught my kid everything I know, and he still acts stupid.
- I don't know if heavy metal music is demonic, but it sure sounds like hell.
- Little boy stopped by living room and said: "I'm go-

ing up to say my prayers now. Anybody want any-
thing?"
■ Mixed emotions is when your teen-ager gets an A in
sex education. - *James Dent*, Charleston, W. Va.,
Gazette
■ My daughter has changed her field of study 12 times.
She is majoring in indecision.
■ My kid ran into a major disappointment last week
while he was looking for a job. He found one.
■ My kids and I have an agreement. I don't tell them
what to do and they don't do it.
■ My kids aren't perfect but I will never forgive the
police for what they did to my kids. They brought
them home.
■ My son gave my wife something for mother's day
that she'll always remember, always treasure, always
be grateful for. He moved out.
■ My son has decided to get a second job. It makes
sense — Its been three years since he quit his first
job.
■ Neighbor's 6-year-old son just got a dog. They are
sending him to obedience school. If it works out,
they'll send the dog, too.
■ On long car trips, I used to play games with my kids.
The best one was called: "What Would You Do If
Daddy Dropped You Off Here?"
■ Our children are the hope of tomorrow – and If you
look real close, you can see tomorrow cringe.
■ Our dog is like a member of the family. I wish I could

say the same about our son.

■ Over the years, I've watched my children grow up from little monsters to full monsterhood.

■ Parents! Have you ever wished that the same person who invented the self-cleaning oven — would now turn his attention to diapers?

■ Play is the work of childhood.

■ Poverty is hereditary – you get it from your children.

■ Pride is what you feel when the kids hold a garage sale and make $143. Panic is what you feel when you realize the car is missing.

■ Show me a home with young children and I'll show you a home where every pack of cards count at between 37 and 51.

■ I solicited money to feed a kid for a month for $10. Then, I sent them there.

■ Some kids are going in for a radical, revolutionary new concept, it's called presexual marriage.

■ Some people say children should be seen and not heard. I disagree. Why should they be seen?

■ Statistics show that the most expensive item in any supermarket shopping cart is a child.

■ Stress is when your son comes home and says he has good news and bad news. The good news is that he is not impotent.

■ Teenagers are the only known mammals that wake up asleep.

■ Teenagers – The hope of tomorrow and the hopelessness of today.

- The advice your son rejected is now being given to your grandson.
- The FBI has more than 10 million fingerprints. So has every home with two or more children in it.
- The first thing a child learns when he gets a new drum is that he is never going to get another.
- The good news is when your son calls you from college and says he's finally going to get a sheepskin. The bad news is finding out it's a seat cover for his car.
- The thing I enjoyed most were visits from children. They did not want public office. – *Herbert Hoover*
- The way kids act today, if you get a divorce and you get custody of the kids — most people figure you lost.
- There never was a child so lovely that his mother was not glad to get him asleep.
- There's a time when you have to explain to your children why they were born - and it's a marvelous thing if you know the reason by then.
- Those who can, do. Those who can't, teach. And those who can't teach - have my son in their class.
- Time does fly. Seems like only yesterday that I was teaching Junior to ride on a bike and it was just yesterday that Junior was teaching me how to run a PC.
- Timid 10-year-old said when he grows up he wants to be exactly like me. I asked what he meant. He said he wanted to be able to yell at kids.
- Today happens to be a very important day for my

son. He's celebrating the second anniversary of his socks.

- My two-year old loves phones. When no one is around he picks up the phone and punches keys. Caught him heading for the phone and made a dive to get him before he hit the keys. He handed me the phone: "It's for you."

- Want to get even with your neighbors who are rich and snobby? Buy their kid a whistle.

- We agreed to have a second child but only because I thought the hospital would take the first one back as a trade-in.

- We cannot give in to terrorists' demands. Anyone who has ever had children knows that.

- We had our kid's baby shoes bronzed — and he still wore them out.

- We have a teenage daughter who lives alone – in our house.

- We insist that our kids learn the value of a dollar and then we wonder why our kids are so depressed.

- We must teach our children to dream with their eyes open.

- We should lower the voting age to fourteen. After all, that's when they know everything.

- We've decided to leave three things to our kids. Number three is our house. The first and second are our mortgages.

- We've finally decided to put our son up for adoption. He's 32.

■ When a kid, I was taught the laws of gravity — shut up and sit down.

■ When I was a toddler, my mother kept telling me, "Walk to grandma! Walk to grandma!" Unfortunately, Grandma lived across the river.

■ Why do children seem to grow up fast and leave home so slowly.

■ Why is the advice you give to a kid considered dumb until he gets the same advice from another kid?

Attorney just chased an ambulance 12 miles and found another lawyer inside.

Lawyers

■ A felon on trial is concerned about his chances. His lawyer tells him: "Be calm. I'm a terrific lawyer. I'll prove to the jury that you were in Hong Kong when the crime was committed. I'll put two doctors on the stand who'll prove you were temporarily insane. I'll pay off two of their witnesses. I have two school buddies on the jury and my wife's uncle is the judge. But just to be on the safe side, if I were you, I'd try to escape.

- A lawyer was awakened by the devil who said: "I am going to give you all the money you can ever spend in exchange for your soul, your wife's soul, the souls of your children and the souls of your parents." Lawyer said: "Sounds good, but what's the catch?"

- America has 70% of the world's lawyers and 70% of the world's ambulances.

- An unscrupulous lawyer for a man arrested for murder, bribed a man on the jury to hold out for a verdict of manslaughter. The jury was out a long time and finally returned with a verdict of manslaughter. The lawyer rushed to the juror. "Here's your money. I'm much obliged to you. Did you have a very hard time?" "I had a hell of a time. The other 11 wanted to acquit."

- As Supreme Court Justice Potter Stuart said of pornography: "I can't define it but I know it when I see it!"

- Caller: "I want to speak to Lawyer Brown." "This is the fifth time you have called this week and I keep telling you Lawyer Brown passed away last week." "I know. I just wanted to hear it one more time."

- Defeated champ Buster Douglas earned $22 million for 7 minutes work. What does he thinks he is, a lawyer?

- Doctor and Lawyer talking. Woman asked doctor about sore knee. He told her about compresses. After she left, the doctor said to lawyer, I think I should send her a bill, don't you? The next day, the doctor sent the woman a bill and the lawyer sent the doctor a bill.

■ Drug lords are being stripped of their wealth — by defense attorneys.

■ Ever wonder how much time you could save by leaving most of your estate to your lawyer?

■ I tried to raise my son right. I taught him to always tell the truth, to avoid bad company and to respect the value of an honest dollar. Yet, in spite of everything, he still enrolled in Law School.

■ A group of lawyers were on a fishing boat and fell in the ocean. The sharks did not eat them! The reason: Professional Courtesy.

■ If law school is so hard to get into, how come there are so many lawyers?

■ If there would be no bad people, there would be no good lawyers.

■ If we all live by 'an eye for an eye' kind of justice, the whole world will be blind. – *Gandhi*

■ Dilemma: If you were locked in a room with (a) a rabid vampire bat, (b) a starved pit bull, and (c) a lawyer — and you had a gun with only two bullets!

■ A judge fined a motorist for speeding and told the driver he would receive a receipt when he paid his fine. Motorist asked if he was supposed to frame it. The judge told him to save three and he would get a bicycle.

■ Ignorance of the law is no excuse. My lawyer practices anyway.

- Instead of sending people to jail, judges are sentencing them to community service. It seems like some of those guys could do their community a big service by moving to another community.
- It's not that there are too many lawyers. There just aren't enough ambulances.
- Lawsuits are getting out of hand. Before I help an old lady across the street, I make her sign a release form.
- Lawyer asked, "Are you sure you told me all the truth? If I am going to defend you I must know everything." Man said he told all. Lawyer said he could get him acquitted due to his alibi, and added, "Are you absolutely sure you told me everything." Man said he told him everything "except where I hid the money."
- Lawyer went to Heaven. St. Peter asked what he did. Lawyer said trial lawyer. Peter said there was a five year wait for civil cases. Lawyer went to explore Hell and found only a two-week delay. Lawyer asked the Devil why. He said: "We got all the judges down here."
- Lawyers are my favorite sub-species.
- Man on crutches told friend he was in accident six months ago. Friend said why are you still on crutches. He says. "I could get along without them...but my lawyer says I can't."
- Motorist asked cop if he could park where he was. Policeman said no. How about these others? They didn't ask.
- Murderers who claim "temporary insanity" should receive a temporary death penalty.

- A New York Mayor wanted to hire 8,000 new cops. To add to the expense, he'll also have to build 400 new doughnut shops.
- Old lawyers never die; they just lose their appeal.
- Old story about the small town lawyer who was starving. Then another lawyer moved to town. Three months later they were both rich.
- Sports store was robbed. The thief was arrested and hired a lawyer. The lawyer said he would not take the case unless he was innocent. The man said he was. He also said he didn't have much money and asked if he could help pay his lawyer with golf balls?
- There are 715,000 lawyers in the U.S. – an increase of 32% over eight years. At this rate, every one in the country will be a lawyer by the year 2223.
- There is one lawyer for every 9,600 people in Japan, compared to one for every 360 in the U.S. Japan has one engineer or scientist for every 25 people, while the U.S. has one for every 100.
- There's a good reason for lawyers. Think of how boring this world would be, without them.
- This guy was screaming, "Get an ambulance. Find me an ambulance!" I asked him if he was hurt, and he said: "No. I just graduated from law school."
- Two sorts of lawyers — the ones who know the law, and the ones who know the judge.
- Use lawyers for medical research, instead of white mice. There are more lawyers and you don't get so attached to them.

■ We all know that when the going gets tough, the tough get lawyers.

■ What do you call a lawyer with an IQ of 50? Your honor.

■ What do you get when you cross a Mafia godfather and an attorney? An offer you don't understand.

■ What's the first thing you should do after running over an attorney? Back up.

■ Why is it that when you need a lawyer, you always can find one?

■ You may have the right to burn the flag, but it doesn't look very good on a resume.

■ Young lawyer noted a big lawyer in a restaurant and asked if he would stop by his table to impress his friends. The big lawyer did and lawyer said: "Not now, (_____) I'm eating."

Losers

- A friend: "Listen — that book I borrowed. It wasn't a first edition or autographed or anything was it?"
- A girl who gets a collect obscene phone call – and accepts it.
- A girl who goes to the doctor for a silicone shot and sits on the needle.
- A girl who puts her bra on backwards and it fits.
- A loser is one who bought a used suit at a charity sale, and found his wife's name and phone number in the pocket.
- A man whose wife gives up sex for Lent — and he doesn't find out about it until Good Friday.
- A scientist who has found a cure for nymphomania.
- At their wedding, his bride showed up with a date.
- *A chill:* Your boss: "Got a minute?"
- Dear Aunt Stella: "After my friend George called to thank me for the linen tea towels, it occurred to me that perhaps you received a package of pornographic tapes…"
- Dear Fred: "Thanks for your thoughtful present of a piece of the Wall. Let's hope the officials in Beijing see fit to release you soon…"
- Dear Rachel: "I write to apologize. I had no idea my

date was lacing your eggnog…"

■ Guest arriving at party: "Hey, who has the silver Mustang that was parked pretty far off the curb?"

■ Her eyes were bright and shining; her skin was soft as rain. She stole my heart, she stole my soul — plus wallet, watch and chain.

■ I can't win. I had a rose delivered to my girlfriend every day for a month. Yesterday she ran off with the delivery man.

■ I said "good morning" and he was stuck for an answer.

■ I went on a diet the day I put my best foot forward and couldn't see it.

■ I've always wanted to be somebody. But I see now I should have been more specific.

■ If he bought a pumpkin farm, they'd call off Halloween.

■ Invested $10,000 in a prize dog for breeding purposes. Found out he barked with a lisp.

■ Its easy to separate winners from losers. Winners know when opportunity knocks and losers knock every opportunity.

■ Got a kidney transplant from someone with a bedwetting problem.

■ Loser is a guy whose brain transplant failed - and nobody noticed.

■ Loser is when you meet a girl at a singles bar wearing a coin charger.

■ Loser when Blue Cross refers you to the Red Cross.

123

- Loser when Book of the Month Club only writes to you once a month.
- Loser when health foods make you ill.
- Loser when your psychoanalyst turns off his hearing aid.
- Loser when your tranquilizers make you nervous.
- Mafia Dish – a broken leg of lamb.
- No drinking problem. Just a stopping problem.
- Rough times. My bank says I'm overdrawn, my boss says I'm overpaid and my wife says she's overdue.
- The best way to collect and serve okra…is to someone else.
- The dentist: "Hmmmmm."
- The East German who spent 12 years digging a tunnel under the Berlin wall.
- The hairdresser: "Now before you look at this in the back, it will look much longer after it's been fluffed up a bit"

Marriage

■ Anyone who says he can see through women is missing a lot. — *Groucho Marx*

■ If we really were honest about what our national sport is, we would drink Gatorade on honeymoons.

■ 40th anniversary for farmer and wife. Farmer said they should celebrate and at least kill a chicken. His wife asked: "Why blame the chicken?"

■ A friend of mine fixed me up with a blind date. I had all but given up on life; I had nothing to live for, now I do – revenge.

■ A good husband remembers his wife's birthday but forgets the year.

■ A mixed marriage. She's Perrier. He's Ripple.

■ A recent poll of women revealed that the number one reason for divorce is men.

■ A successful marriage requires falling in love many times, always with the same person.

■ A woman has a joint checking arrangement with her husband. If he doesn't get home by 1 a.m., she starts checking all the joints.

■ Absence makes the heart go wander.

■ A husband was active in community affairs – until his wife found out.

*Women live longer because they
don't have to marry women.*

■ After all these years of zipping up your wife's dress, have you ever wondered who's zipping her down?

■ Any changes in 50 years of marriage? 50 years ago we called our waterbed "The Sea of Love." Now we call it "The Dead Sea."

■ As Noah said to his wife, "Do me a favor. Quit saying 'into a life some rain must fall.'"

■ Being single means you don't have to leave a party just when you are starting to have a good time.

■ Best way to avoid sex; get married. – *Joey Adams*

- Bridegrooms Anonymous: Whenever I feel like getting married, they send out a lady in a housecoat and hair curlers to burn my toast for me.
- Cheap: Got a note from kidnappers demanding $50,000 for the safe return of his wife. He asked if they had anybody less expensive.
- Couple got married and lived happily even after.
- I'll dance on your grave. Good. I am going to be buried at sea.
- Didn't sleep alone until I got married.
- Divorce expenses are outpacing the inflation rate. The cost of living is less than the cost of leaving.
- Doctor to wife: I don't like the way he looks. Wife: Neither do I, but he's handy around the house.
- Don't want to brag but my wife has a fantastic body. Mine.
- Don't want to say anything about her driving but our second car is a tow truck.
- Sharon Stone is what you're thinking about when your wife says, "What are you thinking about?" and you say, "Nothing."
- He married her because they have so many faults in common.
- He's always been indecisive. At his wedding, when the minister asked "Do you take this woman." He asked, "Can I get back to you on that?"
- He, married 50 odd years. She, 50 very odd years.
- His wife says it's just like being married to Santa Claus. Every night he comes home with a bag on.

- Housework is something you do that nobody notices unless you don't do it
- How do I feel about my ex-husband? I have mixed feeling – a mixture of anger, resentment and disgust.
- How long does it take for a husband to do the dishes? Ten hours. Four minutes to load the dishwasher and nine hours and 56 minutes to take credit for doing them.
- Your husband just slipped under the table. No, my husband just slipped in the door.
- Husband: I feel 10 years younger after I shave in the morning. Wife: Ever think of shaving before going to bed?
- I can pinpoint the exact moment when our marriage went bad. After my wife and I bought a waterbed, we kind of drifted apart
- I had some words with my wife – and she had paragraphs with me.
- I have a second wife. My first developed taste.
- I keep trying to convince my wife that chastity is fattening.
- I often think about marriage – it keeps my mind off sex.
- I used to be my own worst enemy; then I got married.
- I wish my wife would stop referring to my life insurance as "The Big Payoff."
- I'm married to a woman who is everything man could want in an ex-wife.
- I've been married for 41 years, and I'm still in love

with the same woman. If my wife ever finds out, she'll kill me.

■ If science was really on our side, they'd discover that sex cures headaches.

■ If you really want to have a fantastic honeymoon, take it a year after the divorce.

■ It was a short marriage. The divorce papers came while I was finishing my second piece of the wedding cake.

■ It's a friendly separation — he gets to keep whatever falls out of the truck as she drives away.

■ It's not because I found you in bed with my wife. It's because I found you smoking in my house.

■ Just a few words mumbled before the minister and you're married. Just a few words mumbled in your sleep and you're divorced.

■ Kids get married too early these days. I was at a wedding this weekend. For gifts, the bride/groom were registered at Toys-R-Us.

■ Love is blind – marriage is the eye-opener.

■ Love is never having to say you're sorry. Marriage is having to say it all the time.

■ Make sure your husband takes out the garbage. Just put it in his golf bag.

■ Marge and I agree on everything except who we should have married.

■ Marriage has many pains but celibacy has no pleasures.

■ Marriage is the alliance of two people, one who never remembers birthdays and the other who never forgets them.

■ My aunt and uncle were married in 1936. I asked them which years were the best. They said, the ones prior to that.

■ My husband says he's going to a prayer meeting, and then he comes home with a Gideon Bible.

■ My wife said: "I'm leaving you." "Is there another man," he asked. She said: "There's got to be."

■ My wife and I celebrated our 5th anniversary at an elegant restaurant. After dinner, I asked her if she would do it all over again. She said, yes, but I would order the broiled lobster.

■ My wife and I go everywhere together. It's a matter of love, devotion and mutual suspicion.

■ My wife and I keep the Ten Commandments. Five apiece.

■ My wife wore a chastity belt right up until the day we got married - at which time she locked it.

■ A policeman saw an old man crying. The man said he was newly married to a beautiful, perfect young wife. Then why are you crying, the policeman asked? I'm crying because I can't remember where I live.

■ No wonder so many marriages fail. The bride is never the maid of honor - and the groom is never the best man.

■ Now separate vacations: Wife goes where she wants and husband goes where he wants. The old days, wife went where she wanted and the husband went where she wanted.

- On their wedding night, his wife said she wanted to slip into something more comfortable. It was another hotel.

- One of the great mysteries of life is how the idiot who married your daughter can be the father of the smartest children in the world.

- One reason beards have become popular is that it's one of the few things men can do that women can't do better.

- Prescription for a Happy Marriage: Live each day as if it were your last, and each night as if it were your first.

- I'm sad because my wife said she wouldn't speak to me for 30 days and this is the last day.

- She cannot cook, but I don't care. She has such lovely silken hair. She cannot sew, but that's not much. She has the skin I love to touch. She cannot dust but that's okay. She has a kind and gentle way. She cannot stand married life. Which is fine; I already have a wife.

- She gives her husband a voice in everything she buys — an invoice.

- Some say AIDS can't be caught during casual contact. So the answer is simple. Only have casual contact. Get married.

- The worst thing about divorce is you have to be married to get one.

- There are 27 single women where I work who refuse to get married. How do you know? I asked them.

■ They say matches are made in Heaven. Of course. They don't need matches in the other place.

■ "Try these pants," asked the wife. "I can't get into those pants," said her husband. The wife said: "That's right and you won't until you change your ways."

■ Two can live as cheaply as one but only for half as long.

■ We had a happy marriage until she found out that the book of the month club doesn't hold meetings.

■ We went to an X-rated movie. Halfway through we left, drove home and she ran straight to the bedroom – and locked herself in.

■ We would buy a new house but we'd have to use all the money we've been saving for a divorce.

■ We've always had safe sex. It's called a headache.

■ Wife asked why don't we snuggle in the car, like we used to do. Husband: I haven't moved.

■ Man was walking through a cemetery looking for John Murphy's tombstone, but found only Dorothy Murphy's. He asked a woman standing near the stone, about the name. She said, Dorothy Murphy, that's him. Everything's in my name.

■ Wife obeys traffic signs. She saw a sign at McDonald's saying "Drive Through Window" – so she did.

■ Wife taking up belly dancing and wants me to buy her a jewel. Only trouble is she has a 40 carat navel.

■ Wife told husband she couldn't take it anymore and was leaving. "Me either. I'll go with you."

■ Winning isn't everything. If it was, no husband in his

right mind would ever get into an argument with his wife.

■ Woman reporting her missing husband: He is 29, 6 ft., 3 in. and handsome. Desk sergeant said he knew her husband as 48, short and overweight. Woman: Sure he is, but who wants him back.

Medicine

■ I don't mind toughing it out in the dentist's office, but I always ask for a shot of Novocain before I get my bill.

■ Anyone who has ever sat in a doctor's waiting room knows what it's like to be a hostage.

■ Guy came out of doctor's office and said "Thank God! It's only VD."

■ I asked my doctor if I had anything serious. He said, "Only if you have plans for next year."

■ My doctor gave me a very unusual prescription – two aspirins and a plane ticket to Lourdes.

■ My doctor has no objection to house calls as long as you're willing to come to his house.

■ Sometimes it doesn't pay to get rid of stress. I know an executive who was told by his doctor to relax, take the day off and go fishing. He did. Caught a shoe, a tire, a cold and when he got home, he caught his wife with the doctor.

■ With threat of nuclear war, acid rain, crime in the streets and AIDS — hardly pays to quit smoking.

■ If you're at death's door, our doctors will pull you through.

■ A man in the doctor's office was asked to take his

clothes off. He asked the nurse where to put them. She said next to hers.

- Not very good health and accident insurance. If I'm run over by a truck, it pays for damage done to the truck.
- Use Preparation H and kiss your hemorrhoids goodbye.
- When I put a tooth under my pillow at night, the next day I would find a bill from my dentist.
- A friend is working on a cure for dyslexia. He hopes to win a Prilitzer Pull.
- A miracle drug is one that costs the same thing it did last year.
- A psychiatrist told his patient: "I've discovered your problem. You're as nutty as a fruitcake."
- A very considerate dentist. He says, "Let me know if this hurts..." just before he gives me his bill.
- After a long wait in the doctor's office, a man stood up and said: "Well, I guess I'll just go home and die a natural death."
- After my physical, I asked the doctor: "Well, how do I stand?" He said: "That's what puzzles me."
- An optimist is anyone who makes a 10 a.m. appointment with a doctor — and doesn't pack lunch.
- Biggest problem with health foods is that they taste exactly like they look.
- Birth control pill for men, called "No Kids on the Block" or "St. Joseph's Aspirin for No Children."
- Carrying health insurance is like wearing a hospital

gown – you only think you're covered.

■ Children are getting more sophisticated. I heard two six-year-olds talking. One said, "Let's play doctor. You operate and I'll sue."

■ Chiropractor's waiting room is filled with magazines — all back issues.

■ Do you ever have the feeling that the aim of modern medicine is not to keep you from dying, but to keep you alive long enough to pay for modern medicine?

■ Doctor gave his patient six months to live. When he couldn't pay his bill, he gave him another six months. – *Henny Youngman*

■ Doctor making rounds — at golf course.

■ Doctor said jogging could add years to my life. I've jogged for a month and feel 5 years older.

■ Doctor told wife: "I'm worried about your husband. I don't like the way he looks." Wife said: "Neither do I but he's good to the kids."

■ A doctor with ethics always had a third person in room – and called a couple into his office. When he finished examining the woman, she hurriedly dressed and dashed out of the examining room. Doctor said to the man: "Your wife was in a hurry. She'll be fine in a few days." The man said: "She's not my wife. I was wondering why you called me in here with you."

■ Doctor: "I can't find the cause of your illness but frankly, I think it's due to drinking." Patient: "Oh, then I'll come back when you're sober."

■ Some doctors are men who prescribe medicines of

which they know little, to cure diseases of which they know less.

- Dog bit a man. The man said he had rabies — and began writing. He said he would live — and didn't need to write a will, but was making list of people he was going to bite.
- God created the heavens and earth in six days. He could have done it in five, but He stopped on Wednesday to let doctors play through.
- God heals and the doctor takes the fee.
- God said to Moses: "Take two tablets and call me in the morning."
- Good physical condition not only adds years to your life, but life to your years.
- Had a coughing fit in my doctors office. I coughed up 85 bucks.
- Have you noticed that the only person who is never on time for a doctor's appointment - is the doctor?
- He seriously considered going to medical school - to the degree that he purchased a set of expensive golf clubs.
- His parents always wanted him to be a doctor. They figured it was the best way to get back at the hospital that delivered him.
- His rule is never to say "oops" in the operating room.
- Hospital — a place where a patient's friends meet to tell him their symptoms.
- Hospitals work this way – People in the hospital are inpatients, people in their homes are outpatients, and

people in the waiting room are impatient.
- How am I doing on my diet? Read my hips.
- I asked my doctor if he could cure me. He said: "Not on your salary."
- I finally found a health insurance package we can afford. It covers all medical and surgical procedures except those performed by doctors.
- I found an insurance company that only covers minor injuries — Black and Blue Cross.
- I had the flu so bad, I would have died if I'd had the strength.
- I have a family physician. He treats mine and I support his.
- I just had my annual physical and the doctor said I'm sound as a yen.
- I know a medical insurance company that now accepts 10 years in publishing as legal proof of permanent brain damage.
- I once went to a doctor who specializes in acupuncture. I got stuck for $200.
- I put three kids through college - my *dentist's* kids.
- I told my doctor I have a terrible ringing in my ears and asked what I should do. He told me to get an unlisted head.
- I will never understand a doctor who says that what you need is a long rest – when you have just had one in his waiting room.
- I'm all for yogurt, tofu, wheat germ, fish oil and other good healthy things. But, please, not while I'm eat-

- If you ate two apples a day, would that keep two doctors away?
- If you think there is a surplus of doctors, try getting sick during the World Series.
- Losing your memory? Forget it!
- A man had problem with mouth open and gasping for breath and eyes popping out. Doctor said he had three months to live. He went on a spending spree. He went into haberdashery shop and ordered a dozen shirts, size 14 1/2 in the neck and 32 in the sleeves. The salesman said he would measure his neck, and said: "You need size 16. If you took 14 1/2, you'd be going around with your mouth open, gasping for breath and your eyes popping out."
- Man in hospital. There was a knock on the door and a lady doctor came in. She said, "Take off your clothes," and she gave him a complete physical. When she finished, she asked if he had any questions. He said yes, "Why did you knock?"
- Man ran into the doctor's office and said he had a cold, and what did the doctor suggest. Doctor: "I'd suggest you try to get pneumonia. We have a cure for pneumonia but we can't do a thing for a common cold."
- Man throwing a party with champagne and caviar said if his doctor could see him, he'd go crazy. Why, a friend asked, are you on a diet? No, I owe him $500.
- A man told his doctor he wasn't feeling well. Doctor

asked if he smoked (no), drank (no), kept late hours (no). Doctor: how can I cure you if you have nothing to give up.

■ Man with tennis elbow went to acupuncturist who solved problem with three needles in elbow. That evening, he had throbbing pain – and called the acupuncturist and complained that his elbow was killing him. The acupuncturist said: Take two thumbtacks and call me in the morning.

■ Message on prescription to pharmacist: I got mine. Now you get yours.

■ Minor operations are those performed on other people.

■ MRI means Money Reduction Instrument.

■ My doctor told me if I want to stay healthy, I should cut out everything I enjoy — so I told him how much I enjoy paying his bills.

■ My dentist makes me put my money where my mouth is.

■ My doctor finally broke down and agreed to make a house call. It was great. I kept him waiting in my living room for an hour and a half.

■ My doctor has an interesting stress test. It's his bill.

■ My doctor insists that I see him more often. He thinks I'm getting too heavy around the wallet.

■ My doctor said my condition was hereditary. I said: "Fine. Send the bill to my father."

■ My doctor says I have a drinking problem. Not true. I have a stopping problem.

- My doctor told me I am in excellent physical condition, except for my body.
- My doctor wants me to slow down — I was getting well before he could cure me.
- My health insurance is an HMO. That stands for Hand your Money Over.
- My secretary has health problems. She has her appendix removed about every nine months.
- Never trust a doctor who uses the saying: "Malpractice makes perfect."
- Nurse answered phone. Voice said: "I would like to know the condition of Fred Gay. Would you tell me please?" She checked a chart and replied: "He spent a restful night. He's improving steadily. Who shall I say called?" "Well, this is Fred Gay. My doctors won't tell me a thing."
- One advantage in being poor is the doctor will cure you faster.
- Oral Roberts said that if he didn't get 4.5 million dollars, God would take him away. I've had doctors like that.
- Organ transplants are becoming commonplace. My doctor charges labor plus parts.
- Our doctor isn't the kind who takes Wednesdays off to play golf. That's the day he works.
- Our son may grow up to be a doctor. He's already showing a strong interest in expensive cars and golf.
- Patient said he would not insult the doctor by paying him, but had entered a handsome legacy in his will.

Doctor said that was fine but he wanted to look at the prescription again. Wanted to make a small change.

■ Patient to doctor: "How can I ever repay you for your kindness and care?" Doctor: "By check, money order or cash."

■ The art of medicine consists of amusing the patients while nature cures the disease – *Voltaire* (French physician).

■ The doctor cured my insomnia, but now I have to work nights to pay his bill.

■ The doctor said he was in good shape for a man of 50. The trouble was that he was only 40.

■ The government has come up with a radical new plan to reduce medical costs. It wants golf courses to lower their greens fees — and then doctors could pass on the savings to us.

■ The neurotic builds castles in the air. The psychotic lives in them. The psychoanalyst collects the rent.

■ The only person I know of who died from too much salt was Lot's wife.

■ The patient said of his attractive nurse: "Wonderful nurse. One touch of her hand cooled my fever instantly." Doctor said: "I know. I could hear her slap to the end of the corridor."

■ The person who has everything usually sits next to you in the doctor's office.

■ The third day of a diet is not so bad. By then you are off it.

■ The young lady asked the doctor: "Will the scar show?" The doctor said: "That is entirely up to you."

■ They say one in four persons in the U.S. has mental problems. You need not be concerned unless you have three friends that seem perfectly normal.

■ Two optometrists were business partners. They split everything 20-20.

■ Who says that eggs are not good for the heart. Ever seen a chicken with a pacemaker?

■ His doctor told him to give up golf. His golf instructor told him the same thing.

MC (Emcee Liners)

■ I noticed a guy on the ledge on the 40th floor of a skyscraper. I tried talking him down and was partially successful - he jumped from the 20th floor.

■ It's great to see yawns in the audience. At least I

Our next speaker needs no introduction.
Which is fortunate because I've forgotten his name.

know you are still awake.

■ Nothing went right today. A police dog gave me a ticket for parking next to a fire hydrant.

■ There are no embarrassing questions - just embarrassing answers.

■ (Q and A) Who would like to cast the first stone?

■ (Bad joke) I could have timed that joke better. I should have waited until everyone had left the room.

■ (No A/C) Well, the manager had a choice of paying the electric bill, hiring an after-dinner speaker or taking a trip to Florida. Guess which one he chose?

■ (No mike) I've been wanting to say this for a long time – read my lips.

■ (Squealing microphone) Now I know what a dog feels like when he hears a dog whistle.

■ (Bad joke) You had to be there...and I wish I was there right now.

■ (Intro to a big subject) As Roseanne Barr's seamstress says, "We have a lot to cover."

■ (A wonderful introduction) If you still feel that good about me come Christmas I'm partial to Cadillacs.

■ (After long talk) I've often heard (_____) referred to as the 'man of the hour.' Now we all know why.

■ (Crash of glass) I think Ed Meese just broke his specimen jar.

■ (Long speaker) Would the last person to leave the room, please turn off (_____). (Speaker's name).

■ (People walking out) Thank you for that walking ovation.

■ As I look at this award, I can't imagine it going to anyone else — especially since your name's already engraved on it.

■ I truly believe there are places in the universe with intelligent life forms. Unfortunately, Earth isn't one of them.

■ Since I'm parked outside at a meter, we'll be taking a break every 30 minutes.

■ A woman approached me and said she wanted me to be the father of her child. I was flattered until I learned her child was five years old.

■ An emcee is a person who introduces people who need no introduction.

■ At most banquets you'll find more after dinner speakers. Don't look on me as the last speaker, look on me as your wake-up call.

■ Eastern Time, Central Time, Mountain Time. How about waste of time.

■ Either you've heard that joke before or you never want to hear it again.

■ Every after-dinner speech has a happy ending. Everyone is glad it's over.

■ First, let me bring this microphone to the level of the previous comments.

■ Good news only: You are no longer eligible for membership in Weight Watchers...Willard Scott is on vacation...No assembly is necessary and batteries are included...You have been transferred to our Honolulu office...Merry Christmas! Sorry, no time for our annual family newsletter this season.

■ Hope you don't mind if I refer to my notes. I have a photographic memory but it no longer offers same-day service.

■ Heredity runs in my family.

■ Humility has made him a 100% better person.

■ I attended a Mafia birthday party. Everyone went down to the river and bobbed for relatives.

■ I hate junk mail. Today I got 20 envelopes of literature from the Save The Trees people.

■ I have just returned from Boston. It's the only thing to do if you find yourself up there. – *Groucho Marx*

■ I haven't heard that much silence since I asked my wife if I could have a night out with the boys.

■ I just finished by first novel. It went so well, I may even read another one.

■ I think you're going to enjoy our next speaker, but don't hold me to that.

■ I told that joke to break the ice, but I seem to have fallen through.

■ I was a little late tonight. I couldn't find a parking space, and it took me a while to sell my car.

■ I wish I had a hundred jokes like that; unfortunately I've got a thousand.

■ I'd like to thank the previous 29 speakers for whipping you into this frenzy of enthusiasm.

■ I'd ask for a moment of silence for that joke, but you already gave it.

■ I'll pretend I didn't hear that. — *Vincent van Gogh*

- I'm not here to bore you with a lot of statistics. I'm here to introduce you to the person who will.
- I'm not paranoid - ask anyone who is out to get me.
- I've known our speaker since the day he was born – although it seems like longer.
- If God meant man to fly, he would have made it easier to get to the airport.
- If it's such a small world, why is my phone bill so high.
- If the end of the world comes, I hope to be in Cleveland because everything happens there 20 years later.
- In a show of hands, how many people here are opposed to audience participation?
- It's been a long night, so permit me to make it longer.
- Let us begin by closing our eyes, bowing our heads, and saying a silent prayer for all the attempts at humor that will die this evening.
- Light travels faster than sound. That's why some folks appear bright until they speak.
- Man and wife driving home. A cop stopped his car and said he was driving 77 mph. He says no, jumps out of car and grabs the cop. The cop asked his wife if he is always like this. She says only when he is drunk.
- My idea of a perfect vacation is a quaint little cabin in the woods, walking distance to a babbling brook and a casino.
- Nothing goes right. One time I applied for a student loan. They sent me three students.
- Now I know how a tire feels after it's run over a nail.

- On the day he graduated, his father gave him the keys to his business – it had gone bankrupt years before but he still had the keys.

- Our last speaker was a long-time friend. (Look at watch) When he started speaking, he was a brand new acquaintance.

- Our next speaker is widely recognized as one of the best around at what he does. Unfortunately, public speaking is not what he does.

- Please hold your applause until I've introduced all the guests, but you can feel free to boo them individually.

- Show me a home where the buffalo roam and I'll show you a very messy house.

- Sorry I'm late. I got in a small accident, but it wasn't my fault. The guy didn't signal he was parked.

- Studies show the riskiest time for a heart attack is during sleeping hours. I caution you — stay awake during my talk.

- The hotel is the pits. The picture on the wall is of the hotel across the street. You have to put in a quarter to *stop* the bed from vibrating.

- The only way to stay awake during the afterdinner speech is to make it.

- The parking lot was so jammed with cars, I had to drive around until one was stolen.

- The story you are about to hear is true. The names have been changed to protect me.

- The time to stop talking is before people stop listening.

- This is an unexpected turnout. Are you sure you're all in the right room?
- Three secrets to public speaking — be sincere, be brief, be seated.
- We saw a man dig a woman's car out of the snow. The age of shovelry is not dead.
- A toastmaster is someone who keeps popping up with a crummy joke.
- Amazing how noisy an audience is when you ask for quiet - and how quiet it can be when you ask for money.
- And now, as any prudent doctor would advise, it's time for a second opinion.
- Every speaker has a mouth. An arrangement rather neat. Sometimes its filled with wisdom. Sometimes it's filled with feet.
- Every toastmaster feels like a eunich in a harem. He'd like to be the main attraction only he's not cut out for it.
- Haven't been so nervous since I took my Navy physical — and the doctor was carrying a purse.
- Humor is the foreplay of speeches.
- I can tell you right now that's a better question then the answer you're going to get.
- I have my own stable of writers. They can't afford to live in a house.
- I just figured out why the average prayer takes 30 seconds and the average conference three days. God

listens.

- I was going to talk about the future but the future has already come and gone this evening.
- I'm sure we could listen to so-and-so forever. And I think we have.
- Lost dog: Limps from broken hip, blind in one eye. Answers to the name, Lucky.
- Nice to be among friends – even if they are not yours.
- People's number one fear is having to make a speech. Number two fear is having to listen to one.
- President Clintom told me not to name-drop.
- Speakers'dictionary: Fee means money. A negotiated fee means less money. An honorarium means bus fare.
- The next speaker needs no introduction — which is fortunate because I've misplaced the one they gave me.
- They say George Washington could never tell a lie. Which could explain why they didn't ask him to introduce (_____).
- This audience looks like you have been told that laughing is fattening.
- This is a return engagement for me. I was here this afternoon.
- Timing is when you come to the end of your speech before the audience comes to the end of their rope.
- Tonight we'll be talking about our guest of honor's favorite subject – himself.
- What can I say about the previous speakers? Halfway through my foot fell asleep and I can't tell you how

much I envied it.

■ When you follow (_____), you have to watch where your step.

■ Whenever I tell these jokes, I get carried away — and before I am...

Miscellaneous Facts

■ A Neptune year is the time it takes the planet to revolve once around the sun – 164.8 years.

■ Disco, Wis. and Waltz, Mich.; Carefree, Ariz. and Panic, Pa.; Normal, Ill. and Peculiar, Mo.; Sunrise, WY and Sunset, La.; Lively, Va. and Drab, Pa.; Why, Ariz. and Whynot, Miss.

■ How much is a billion dollars? If you spent $1,000 a day, it would take you nearly 3,000 years to spend it all.

■ Only three U.S. patents were granted in 1790 when the Patent Office opened. The first was awarded to Samuel Hopkins of Vermont for "a new method of making pot and pearl ashes." Potash is used in making soap.

■ The size of a human cell is to that of a person as a person's size is to that of Rhode Island. A virus is to a person as a person is to the earth. An atom is to a person as a person is to the earth's orbit around the sun.

■ This decade will have 315,532,800 seconds (including leap years in 1992 and 1996), 17 Friday the 13ths, the average TV user will watch 25,659 hours (1,069 days or 2.9 years), the average man will spend 4,745 hours (nearly 198 days) eating and the average woman will eat 4,442 hours or 185 days.

■ A bakers dozen. In Middle Ages, bakers suffered severe penalties if caught selling bread below legal weight - so they added an extra loaf to play safe.

■ A common fly is faster — in one sense - than a jet airplane. The fly moves 300 times its body length in one second. The jet, at the speed of sound, travels 100 times its body length in one second.

■ A robin has about 3,000 feathers.

■ A white elephant relates to kings of Siam who gave white elephants to courtiers who annoyed them. The animals were sacred and upkeep so costly that anyone who received one was apt to be ruined.

■ Chairman comes from a custom in the Middle Ages where the master of the house and his lady were the only ones who occupied or owned chairs. The others in the household sat on stools or cushions at a lower level.

■ Cost of cup of coffee (average price in hotels) – Tokyo $4.32; Milan $3.58, London $3; Paris $2.42; Sydney $2.36; Athens $2.06; Munich $1.65; Bangkok $1.55; Bejing $1.27; St. Maarten $1.24; Honolulu $1.21; San Juan $1.18; Chicago $1.13; Los Angeles $1.13; Montreal $1.13; Moscow $1.07; New York $1.03; Miami $.91; Mexico City $.74; Nairobi $.62; Sao Paulo $.56; Cairo $.53.

■ Death: On an average day, approximately 140,000 people die in the United States.

■ Don't need a car anymore. There are so many people who want to take you for a ride.

■ Earth was formed 4.6 billion years ago. In the first

4.599 billion years, nothing much happened. In the next million, man invented use for his arms, legs and his cave. In the next 100,000 years, he invented language, tools, the wheel, fire, primitive warfare and agriculture. 5,000 years later, he had invented recorded history, chariots and the Dark Ages. The next 500 he invented gunpowder, printing, the steam engine and the Industrial Revolution, but in the last 100 years, he invented everything else!

■ Gas company cut off Thomas Edison's gas. "I was in the midst of certain very important experiments, and to have the gas company plunge me into darkness made me so mad that I at once began to read up on gas technique and economics, and resolved I would try to see if electricity couldn't be made to replace gas and give those gas people a run for their money."

■ *Get up on wrong side of the bed.* It's unlucky to get out of left side (which was associated by sun setting in the west and symbolizing death).

■ Girl Scout Cookies were first baked in Philadelphia in 1932 by scouts during a cooking demonstration at the corner of Broad and Arch Streets.

■ He was a bold man that first ate an oyster. *– Jonathan Swift*

■ Henry Ford forgot to put a reverse gear in first car he invented. He also didn't have a door opening big enough to get the car outside, once built.

■ Henry Ford founded Ford Motor Company in 1903 with $28,000 raised from selling stock. The company had 12 workers. The first car, the Model T, was sold in 1908 for $850 and could go 40 mph. By 1916, Ford was able to bring the price down to $360.

■ Henry Ford invented charcoal briquettes to make camping more enjoyable with Thomas Edison and Harvey Firestone.

■ Horatio Alger wrote novels. Unsatisfied with writing, he moved from job to job and eventually suffered a breakdown and died broke.

■ How much is a billion? Number of people who claim they were at Woodstock...Food products made with oat bran...How many people who have seen Elvis at K-Mart...Total number of doughnuts eaten by police officers in one year.

■ In classical times, Athens never had a population of much over 100,000 and the average population of Rome was about half a million.

■ In the USA, there are 56 telephones for every 100 people. In Washington, DC, however, there are 130 telephones for every 100 people.

■ JC Penney's name - James Cash Penney. Started a small store in Kemmerer, Wyoming, in 1902.

■ Kick the bucket. Bucket refers to bucket beam or wood frame on which pigs were hung after slaughter.

■ O.K. was first uttered in the 1840 presidential campaign, when Martin Van Buren ran and was nicknamed Old Kinderhook after his birthplace. OK became the rallying cry. Van Buren lost but OK won.

■ Once in a blue moon. During volcanic eruption of

Krakatoa (Indonesia) in 1883, the dust caused the moon to appear blue. Once in a blue moon (American version) – second full moon in the same month. (Happens only once every 2.72 years.)

■ One out of every 167 people has an extra rib. It's usually close to the neck and sometimes causes pain in the shoulder and arm. About twice as many women as men are so endowed.

■ Parachutes were invented more than 100 years before the airplanes. They were created in France in 1783 to save people who had to jump from burning buildings.

■ Pig in a poke. Old time markets displayed pigs for sale and sold them in a bag or poke — which sometimes didn't contain a pig.

■ President Thomas Jefferson invented the swivel chair in 1803. He also invented the folding chair, the lazy Susan, the pedometer and the improved plow.

■ Roman statues were made with detachable heads so that they could be interchanged.

■ Saved by the bell. A 17th century sentry was accused of being asleep, and was court martialed. He claimed he heard the St. Paul's clock strike 13 at midnight.

■ Seven shuffles to mix a deck of cards.

■ Shopping carts. Sylvan Goldman invented the modern day shopping cart in 1937 after observing that shoppers in his Oklahoma City Food Store stopped shopping when their wicker baskets became too full or too heavy.

- Sleep: The average person spends about 220,000 hours asleep during his or her lifetime.
- Some people approach every problem with an open mouth. - *Adlai Stevenson*
- Table cloths were originally meant to serve as towels for guests who wanted to wipe hands and face.
- The annual salary for each President from George Washington to U.S. Grant (1789-1869) was $25,000. From Grant to Theodore Roosevelt's term (1873-1901) it was raised to $50,000. Richard Nixon (1968) was the first president to receive an annual salary of $200,000.
- The basketball dribble was first used by Bert Loomis in 1896.
- The first crossword puzzle was compiled by Arthur Wynne and published in *The New York World* on December 21, 1913. It was based on a parlor game his grandfather taught him known as magic square. Wynne simply separated the words with black spaces and added a list of 32 clues, mostly definitions.
- The first TV commercial was broadcast by WNBT in New York on July 1, 1941. The ad was for a Bulova watch and the 20-second commercial cost $9.00.
- The Internal Revenue Service was founded by President Lincoln on July 1, 1862, to finance the civil war. At that time, the withholding tax applied only to top government employees and only on selected interest and dividends.
- The left leg of a chicken is generally more tender than

the right. A chicken sleeps on its right leg which develops tougher tendons and muscles.

■ The perfect gift for a person who has everything is a burglar alarm. – *Lou Gerber*

■ The term "bring home the bacon" was first used in England in the 1200s. It was for an award to a husband and wife who proved they had lived in greater harmony and fidelity than any other couple.

■ The USA now has 5% of the world's population and 70% of its lawyers. Washington, DC has one lawyer for every 22 people.

■ Traffic lights were introduced in 1920 by a Detroit policeman, Officer William Pots.

■ Umbrellas originated in Mesopotamia 3,440 years ago as an extension of the fan. They were to protect from the sun. Umbrella is from the Latin umbra, meaning shade. They became popular for the rain in the 1780s.

■ When Charles Lindbergh landed at Le Bourget airport, he is quoted as saying, "Well, I made it!" What he actually said was, "Are my mechanics here? ...followed by "Does anybody here speak English?"

■ During production of *The Diary of Anne Frank*, played by Pia Zadora, in the scene where Nazis burst in, someone in the audience shouted, "She's in the attic!"

■ The first dentist, Peter de la Roche, opened his practice in London in 1661. Prior to that, dentistry was a sideline practiced by barbers, blacksmiths and veterinarians.

I've invested heavily in an Atlantic City casino —
a quarter at a time.

Money

■ A bad economy is when you're not doing as well as when you weren't doing well.

■ A fool and his money are soon parted. Of course, that still leaves him with his credit cards.

■ A fool and his money are soon spotted. - *Grit*

■ A group of robbers broke into the Bank of Israel and escaped with 3 1/2 million dollars in pledges.

■ A study of economics usually reveals that the best time to buy something is last year.

■ A vacation resort advertises all the comforts of home. The staff tries to make you feel at home, and the prices make you wish you were home.

- An easy way to defrost my refrigerator every three or four months, I forget to pay my electric bill.
- Anyone who says money can't buy happiness doesn't know how to shop.
- As they say on Wall Street, when the going gets tough, the tough get going — to psychiatrists, stress clinics and Brazil.
- A banker called on an oilman about his loans. The oilman said the wells went dry. He said, "It could have been worse." He drilled new wells and they went dry. He said, "It could have been worse." The banker said, "How could it have been worse?" The oilman said, "It could have been my money."
- Banker – a person who lends you his umbrella when the sun is shining – yet wants it back the minute it rains.
- Bankruptcy is a legal proceeding in which you put your money in your pants pocket and give your coat to your creditors.
- Bankruptcy protects a business and permits it to continue to do all the things that got them into trouble in the first place.
- Banks in trouble. I asked a teller to check my balance — and she leaned out and pushed me.
- Banks lend billions to Third World countries but for us they chain down the pens.
- Banks want a mountain of collateral before they'll lend you a molehill of money.
- Double your money. Fold it over and put it in your

pocket.

■ Due to inflation, a bird in the hand is now worth three in the bush.

■ Farmers are always griping about something – not enough rain, too much rain, an early frost, a late frost, it's too hot, it's too cold. Why don't they stop complaining and just get their meat, fruit and vegetables at the supermarket like the rest of us?

■ FDIC — the Find Dumb Investments Corporation.

■ Fight inflation. Burn a bra.

■ Financial security is that period between the last payment and the first repair bill.

■ Girl used to charge $20 for the key to her room. Not to get in: to get out.

■ Have you ever wondered why it's called instant credit when what it really means is instant debt?

■ Have you ever wondered why they're called down payments when they keep going up?

■ He looks like the guy at the bank – just before he turns down your loan.

■ How come we trust banks with our money, but they can't trust us with their pens?

■ I always feel let down the day after Christmas. It's the first day of the rest of my payments.

■ I been rich and I been poor. Rich is better. — *Sophie Tucker*

■ I bought my new home through Century Twenty-one — and I won't get through paying it off till the end of the 21st Century.

- I don't like money actually, but it quiets my nerves. - *Joe Louis*
- I have a cash flow problem – all my cash has flown.
- I invested in one of those treasure ship salvage companies. So far, their most profitable discovery was me.
- I know a way to become a millionaire — invest two million in penny stocks.
- I own a large portfolio of penny stocks. Of course, they weren't that way when I first bought them.
- I read about a professional fund-raiser who died. In his will, he left his family three million dollars — in pledges.
- I really don't mind paying a graduated income tax. What bothers me is the annual reunions.
- I think my bank is in danger of going under. This Christmas they gave out six-month calendars.
- I was wondering if wealthy Swiss people put their money in American banks?
- I'd like to live like a poor man with lots of money. - *Pablo Picasso*
- I'm part of a unique group insurance policy. The insurance company only pays if the whole group gets sick at the same time.
- I've finished my taxes. It's a great load off my wallet.
- If all the rich men in the world divided up their money among themselves, there wouldn't be enough to go around.
- If anyone calls with a stock tip: Just Say NO.
- Stock Market Crash. What bothered me is that I went

from rich to poor so fast, I skipped "being comfort-able" altogether.

■ If you think modern art is obscene, you should see the price tags.

■ If you're poor, you slip through the cracks. If you're rich, you slip through the loopholes.

■ Income tax is the fairest tax of all. It gives everybody an equal chance at poverty.

■ Inflation is not so bad. It lets every American live in a more expensive neighborhood without moving.

■ It helps to think of the IRS as a speed bump on the road to riches.

■ It's not the bulls and bears on Wall Street that make you lose money. It's the bum steers.

■ Let's all be happy and live within our means, even if we have to borrow money to do it.

■ A man hit by car was lying in the street waiting for an ambulance. A woman covered him with her jacket and propped his head up. She asked: "Are you comfortable?" He replied: "I make a living."

■ Man invented the wheel. And it was a big hit until someone invented the sticker price.

■ A man plunked down a quarter on street stand but didn't take any pretzel. This went on every day for weeks. The woman who had the stand stopped him one day. He said: "You probably want to know about my leaving you a quarter every day." Woman said: "Not at all. I just want to tell you that the price is now 50 cents."

- Maybe money can't buy happiness, but neither can poverty.
- Money is the root of all good.
- Money talks – but who can understand Japanese?
- Most American families have everything. They just haven't paid for it all yet.
- Most of us would be glad to pay as we go, if we could catch up on where we've been.
- Next to being shot at and missed, nothing is quite as satisfying as an income tax refund.
- Nobody ever lost money taking a profit.
- Nothing makes people go into debt like trying to keep up with those who already are.
- Nothing puts a family in debt as much as a raise.
- Now I know why they call them brokers. I'm broker now than before I met him.
- One way to stop all those traffic jams would be to allow on the streets only those automobiles that have been paid for. - *Will Rogers*
- The Pentagon is a five-sided building. Each side faces our wallets.
- A pig and a cow were arguing about which of them make the greatest contribution to man. The pig said he gave man ham, pork and lard. The cow said, she gave milk, cream and butter. That's good said the pig, but when I give, I make a total commitment!
- Pressure is when you've got 35 bucks riding on a four-foot putt and you've only got five dollars. - *Lee Trevino*

- Real estate was so bad that he was playing Monopoly and none of the houses sold.
- Recession. Appliance stores have begun offering free savings accounts to anyone who buys a toaster.
- Salesman tried to convince woman to buy an expensive freezer. Salesman said it would pay for itself in no time at all. She said: Fine. As soon as it does, send it over.
- Show me the man who says money can't buy happiness and I'll show you a man who doesn't get out much.
- Someday we will eat off golden plates. Wife: Will it taste any better?
- Store sent a note that said their bill was one year old. He responded with a note that said: Happy Birthday.
- The average person has two ambitions. To get into heaven in the next life, and to get out of debt in this life.
- The best place to spend your vacation is somewhere near your budget.
- The Eiffel Tower is the Empire State Building after taxes.
- The good news – a stock I owned split. The bad news – so did my broker.
- The government spent so much money to bail out Texas banks that it gave new meaning to the phrase "Texas Panhandle."
- The income tax has made more liars out of the American than golf has. – *Will Rogers*

- The new Infiniti cars are named that because the payments go on forever.
- The new Wall Street Golden Rule: Sell unto others before they have a chance to sell unto you.
- The test of generosity is not how much you give, but how much you have left.
- These days, our dollars go further than ever — all the way to Japan.
- They say money talks; the only thing I hear it saying is goodbye.
- Though there's a limit to what man can use, there is no limit to what he can waste.
- Three banks went under — and so did two toaster companies.
- Time isn't money. Money is money.
- To discourage people from filling out withdrawal slips, my bank installed pens with one-inch chains.
- Today I am the world's happiest sailing enthusiast – I just sold my boat.
- The Wall Street crash created strange sights like seeing someone rowing a yacht.
- Went to a movie. Discovered the cops were on the screen and the robbers were behind the refreshment counter in the lobby.
- What do you call a guy who has missed 10 car payments? A pedestrian.
- What's the difference between a yuppie stockbroker and a pigeon? The pigeon can still make a deposit on a BMW.

- When a man says money can't do everything, it means he doesn't have any.
- When a person tells you he got rich through hard work, ask him whose?
- When I applied for a bank loan, I knew right away I was in trouble. All the employees were wearing "Just Say No" buttons.
- When I was young, I used to think money was the most important thing in life; now that I'm old, I know it is. — *Oscar Wilde*
- When you make out your income tax return, remember that it's better to give than to deceive.
- You can't take it with you, but then, that's not the place where it comes in handy.
- You have to admire rich people for not squandering their money on taxes.
- You really have to hand it to the IRS. If you don't, they come and get it.
- There was a time in my life when I spent 90% of my money on booze and broads. And the rest of it, I just wasted.
- It's good to have money and the things money can buy, but its good to check once in a while and make sure you haven't lost the things that money can't buy.

My Friend Marge

- "I've given you the best years of my Life." "Those were the best?"
- I'm a little tired. Marge and I have a policy that we never go to bed angry. I haven't had any sleep in two weeks.
- After three years of dating, I'd spent so much money on her that I figured I'd marry her for my money.

When we wanted to punish the kids,
we sent them to bed with supper.

- At our house, the dog doesn't beg for food.
- Her idea of a gourmet meal is adding oregano to a TV dinner.
- I bought her a cookbook the day we got married…its still in the wrapper.
- I lied on my taxes again. I listed myself as "head of household."
- I think my wife is laundering money, because my bank account's cleaned out.
- I told Marge that men like Sylvester Stallone and Arnold Schwarzenegger are a dime a dozen. She said: "Here's 5¢. Get me six."
- Marge said she would divorce her husband if she could find a way to do it without making him happy.
- Marge and I had an agreement for my retirement, I would not try to run her life and I would not try to run mine.
- Marge and I have been married for 48 years, and not once has she thought of divorce. Murder, yes, but not divorce.
- Marge has come up with a great device for keeping the kitchen spotless. We eat out.
- Marge is always complaining about toys lying around the house. I can see her point. We don't have any children in the house.
- Marge said if she couldn't handle my being around the house a lot, she would get a job – for me.
- Marge went through a lot with me — my wallet, my bank account, my IRA…

■ Marge wouldn't have any trouble living off the land — providing that land had a shopping mall on it.

■ Marge said that Mark Twain was asked what the people of the world would be like without mothers. He replied: "Scarce, very scarce."

■ Marge said the most remarkable thing about her mother is that for 30 years she served the family nothing but leftovers and no original meal has ever been found.

■ Marge said her mother got angry one year when she forgot Mother's Day and she told her it was an accident. And her mother said: "So were you."

■ Not much of a cook. Her way of helping out in the kitchen is to stay in the dining room.

■ On our anniversary, I wanted to renew our vows. She wanted to let them expire.

■ On our last anniversary, Marge and I went to the same hotel that we went to on our wedding night. The only difference was that the next morning, Marge hung a sign on the door that said: "Disturb."

■ She puts a small and large roast in the oven. When the small one burns, the big one is done.

■ She bought three things marked down — two dresses and an escalator.

■ She fixes Thanksgiving Dinner the old-fashioned way: she burns it.

■ She made me a millionaire. I had two million when we met.

■ At a silent auction I go around and erase her bid —

and don't tell her.

■ Some women carry mace in their purse to discourage attackers. Marge just packs a couple of her salmon patties.

■ The one thing we have in common is that we were married on the same day.

■ The only woman I know who was mugged by Betty Crocker.

■ Three basic food groups – canned, frozen and take-out.

■ To save energy, she keeps the oven at 68 degrees.

■ We pray *after* meals.

■ We were always arguing about a night out with the boys. I didn't think she should have one.

■ When I asked Marge if she could learn to love me, she asked how much I was willing to spend on her education.

■ When Marge is away, she worries about her house plants. If she's not there, who's going to kill them?

■ I used to be indecisive, but now I'm not so sure.

Newspapers

■ A free press is the unsleeping guardian of every other right that free men prize; it is the most dangerous foe of tyranny. – *Winston Churchill*

■ There was an article in the paper about woman who found a snake coiled under her newspaper on the porch. She said she was not surprised at the snake but that the paper was on her porch.

■ A newspaper carrier asked a customer to renew his subscription. The man said he had no time to read and he has been taking paper from porch to rubbish can. The carrier said that he would deliver it straight to rubbish can.

■ A boy delivering groceries was greeted at the door by a lady in a negligee. "Oh," she said, "I thought you were the paper boy." He quit his job with the grocery and took a paper route. He's been in the newspaper business ever since.

■ I don't like journalism. I like news. — *Sen. Jesse Helms*

■ If some great catastrophe is not announced every morning, we feel a certain void. If we have no one in the paper today, we sigh.

■ Journalism consists of buying white paper at 2 cents a pound and selling it at 10 cents a pound. — *Charles*

Dana (1819-97)

■ Most of today's news is too true to be good.

■ My son wants to be an editor but he can't spell, punctuate, construct sentences or use proper grammar. I think he's going to make it.

■ Newspaper sent notice to Ralph Smith that his subscription had expired. The notice came back with a handwritten note, saying: "So has Ralph."

■ One of the great mysteries in life is how a paperboy can pitch a no-hitter in a little league baseball game, but can't hit a front porch with a newspaper.

■ President Bush said puppies in the White House slept on the *New York Times* and *Washington Post,* "marking the first time in history that those newspapers have been used to prevent leaks."

■ Reporter was sent out to investigate a report that a local man could sing the entire score of Aida while eating a seven course meal. Came back and did not write the story. Told editor there is nothing to it. "The guy's got two heads."

■ Sam Donaldson (ABC White House correspondent) traveling in India: In one village, the natives had solved their energy problem by throwing cow manure into a large pit then siphoned off the methane gas to light the village lamps. Sam to President Jimmy Carter: "If I fell in, you'd pull me out wouldn't you, Mr. President," Sam joked. "Certainly," Carter replied. "After a suitable interval."

■ Stop the presses. It's not running.

- Supercarrier is the kid who delivers the Sunday paper.
- The mission of a modern newspaper is to comfort the afflicted and afflict the comfortable.
- The motto of the Washington press corps is: "If you don't have anything nice to say, let's hear it."
- To a newspaper man, a human being is an item with skin wrapped around it. - *Fred Allen*
- Today's journalists are not reaching new lows. They're just reaching old lows more often.
- Why is a newspaper 10 times more interesting when somebody across the table is reading it?
- Circus came to small town. A local newspaper writer wrote about elephants and warned they sometimes relieved themselves – "about a bushel."
- What carries 30 million bits of information, weighs less than 3 pounds, prints hard copy, handles text and graphics, is available 24 hours a day, is completely portable and costs less than 50 cents.

Oldsters

■ ... you decide to procrastinate but never get around to it

■ ... you finally reach the top of the ladder and find it leaning against the wrong wall.

■ ... you get your exercise acting as pall bearer for your friends who exercise.

■ ... you hurt everywhere, and what doesn't hurt, doesn't work.

■ ... you look forward to a dull evening.

■ ... you remember Dr. Pepper when he was an intern.

■ ... you remember when the type on menus was a good deal larger.

■ ... you remember when they gave you a 12-month warranty on your car and you didn't need it.

- ... you sink your teeth in a steak and they stay there.
- ... you sit in a rocking chair but can't get it going.
- ... you still carry a picture of Veronica Lake in your wallet.
- ... your back goes out more than you do.
- ... your birthday cake caves in from the weight of the candles.
- ... your little gray haired lady who helped you across the street is your wife.
- A ninety year old man was placed in a nursing home. He leaned left and a nurse rushed to straighten him. He leaned right, a nurse straightened him again. He leaned forward – same nurse! He told his son, the home was fine, but they wouldn't let him pass wind!
- Adolescence: when you think you'll live forever. Middle age: when you wonder how you've lasted so long.
- Anybody who can still do at 60 what he was doing at 20 wasn't doing much at 20.
- At my age, the best part of waking up isn't Folger's in my cup. It's waking up.
- Big challenge in our society today is to get older women to admit their age and to get older men to act their age.
- During his physical the doctor asked a 70-year old man how old his father was when he died. "Who said he's dead? In fact, he's getting married." Why would he want to do that the doctor asked. "Who said he wants to?"

- Every man desires to live long; yet no man desires to be old. - *Jonathan Swift*
- Everything up to age 40 is just practice.
- First bifocals. First time I ever fell up the stairs.
- For every man at age 74, there are 14 women available to him. Useless information.
- Growing old is a road we must all travel — but it's amazing how many people try to make a U-turn at 40.
- He never smokes, drinks, goes to movies or night clubs. He never swears or plays cards, and he never married. And tonight he's going to celebrate his 89th birthday. How?
- He won't chase women unless it's downhill.
- How old are you? That's my business. You must have been in business a long time.
- I don't fall down as fast as I used to.
- I don't mind growing old — but my body is taking it badly.
- I never believe anyone over the age of 50 who tells me they run, ski, golf and play tennis, handball and racquet-ball – unless they are in the emergency room.
- I won't say how old he is but I counted 72 candles on his last birthday cake and that was my slice alone.
- If you stop to think about it, half the things you say you can't do anymore – are things you never could do.
- If you are old enough to know better, you're too old to do it. - *George Burns*

- If you don't care how old you are, you're young. If you lie about how old you are, you're middle age. And If you brag how old you are, you're *old*.
- It you wish to be successful, talk to three old men. – *Chinese proverb*
- Just one of those days — for years now.
- Just remember, when you're over the hill, you begin to pick up speed.
- Life begins at forty. Begins to what?
- Lit candles on the cake and the air conditioning came on.
- Middle age is when you know all the answers. Nobody ever asks the questions.
- Middle age is when your classmates are so gray and wrinkled and bald they don't recognize you.
- Middle age is when everything is half-paid for.
- Middle-age is when you look into the mirror and wish you hadn't looked into the mirror.
- Middle-age is when you slowly turn from stud to dud.
- Middle-age is when you try to convince yourself it's only the weather.
- My feeling about eulogies is — they're better to give than to receive.
- No longer "senior citizen." Now its "chronologically gifted."
- Old age and treachery will over come youth and skill every time.
- Old age is when you know all the answers, but can't remember why you're taking the test.

- Old age is when your class reunion is called off because the other guy can't make it.
- Old is when your baby pictures are found on cave walls.
- Old man says to young girl: Where have you been all my life? She replied: Well, for the first 45 years, I wasn't even born yet.
- Old people know more about being young than young people know about being old.
- People tell me I don't look my age, but I'm not sure if they mean I look younger or older.
- She's old. Wants to raise the *Titanic* to get her stuff back.
- Some people lie about their age but she is very open and honest about it. She just comes right out and tells you – that it's none of your business.
- Student to old man: Math is an exact science. Figures never lie. The old man said: If a man can build a garage in 12 days, would 12 men build a garage in one day. Then 288 men could build a garage in one hour, 17,280 in a minute and 1,036,80 men could build a garage in one second...?
- Suppository in ear? Now I know what I did with my hearing aid.
- Take all the experience and judgment of men over 50 out of the world and there wouldn't be enough people left to run it. – *Henry Ford*
- The first sign of aging is when you go into a restaurant, ask to see the menu — and realize you can't see

the menu.

- The older we are, the greater we were.
- The young man knows the rules, but the old man knows the exceptions. — *Oliver Wendell Holmes*
- The young want to change the world. The old want to change the young.
- Three stages of men. Tri weekly, try weekly and try weakly.
- To avoid old age, keep over-drinking, over-eating and over-achieving.
- Too old to set a bad example, so he has started to give good advice.
- Used to be a go-getter. Now it takes two trips.
- When you are old and say you never felt better it means that your memory is failing you, too.
- When you decide to go out but you don't know why.
- You are getting old when you attend an antique auction and four people bid on you.
- You don't stop laughing because you grow old; you grow old because you stop laughing.
- You feel like the morning after the night before, and you haven't even been anywhere.
- You know you're getting old when you can't remember the first time you made love, or the last time you made love.
- You know you're getting old when you take a stroll down memory lane and you get lost.
- You know you're getting old when your knees buckle, but your belt won't.

■ You're getting old when it takes you longer to rest up than it did to get tired.

■ You're not very old when your hair turns gray. You're not very old when your teeth decay. But you really are headed for that final sleep, when your mind makes a date that your body can't keep.

■ You're only young once but you can be immature forever.

■ Young man: "What's life's heaviest burden?" Old man: "To have nothing to carry."

Opening Lines

■ The long and short of giving a speech is – the shorter the speech, the longer the applause.

■ After applause) Thank you. You're what every speaker dreams of, a kinder, gentler audience.

■ (After applause) What can I say? You took the words right out of my mother's mouth.

■ (If late) Tonight I shall disprove the old adage, "Better late than never."

■ (Morning meeting) You all look so rested — like you just got back from a night on the town.

■ After very good speaker, Adali Stevenson said: I was sitting next to Fred Allen and during the dinner, I looked at his speech and he looked at mine, and we thought it might be fun if we exchanged speeches. I am very pleased you enjoyed hearing my speech. Now I would like to read Fred Allen's...

■ An Episcopalian bishop was the speaker at dinner. A waiter spilled hot split pea soup on the bishop's lap. The bishop cried out: "Will some layman please say something appropriate to the occasion!"

■ Be careful of the words you say. Keep them soft and sweet. You never know from day to day, Which ones you'll have to eat.

■ Before getting this program underway, let me just

remind everyone that a little boredom never hurt anyone.

- Bill Moyers (Lyndon Johnson's press secretary) was saying grace at a White House dinner. Johnson at end said he had trouble hearing. "Speak up," he said, "I can't hear you." Moyers: "I wasn't talking to you."
- Famous First Words: Adam – "It's a jungle out there." Alexander Graham Bell — "I've been disconnected." Aesop - "That reminds me of a story" Gerald Ford – "OOPS." Stephen King — "Boo!" Mickey Mouse – "Why am I wearing gloves?"
- First, I want you to know that I have a mind of my own. My wife told me to say that.
- (Following a good speaker) If it's true that laughter is the best medicine -_____ has to be considered a wonder drug.
- (Following a good speaker) The rest of us on the program drew lots to see who would follow that — and obviously I lost.
- For those of you who came here tonight expecting a long, drawn out presentation, I won't disappoint you.
- I always appreciate a nice introduction. At least, I always did until a short time ago when I heard that there are two kinds of speakers – those who need no introduction — and those who don't deserve one. Well, now we all know which category I fit in. But don't misunderstand me — I'm grateful for any introduction I get whether I deserve it or not and I'm grateful to you for giving me this opportunity to speak

on a subject I care about.

- I am here for one reason only — and as soon as I find out what that reason is, I'm going home.
- I deeply wish my parents could have been here. My father would have enjoyed what you have so generously said of me – and my mother would have believed it. – *Lyndon Johnson*
- I don't mind working a 10 hour day, but not before noon.
- I have a tendency to ramble. So please don't hesitate to yawn.
- I have always been short, but today I'll try to be brief.
- I have an announcement to make for those of you who left your cars with the valets. Contact the police. The hotel does not have valets.
- I have been given compliments myself a great many times, and they always embarrass me. I always feel that they have not said enough. – *Mark Twain*
- I have to be honest. That introduction was so flattering, so extravagant, so laudatory — it would have embarrassed me if I didn't happen to know that every word of it is true.
- I haven't seen this small an audience since I spoke to the Mensa group in Congress.
- I know you didn't expect to see me. If it makes you feel any better, I didn't expect to see you either.
- I make it a practice after an introduction like that never to say I don't deserve it. I figure you will find

that out soon enough for yourself.

■ I understand that my job is to talk to you. Your job is to listen. But if you quit work before I do, I hope you'll let me know.

■ I wasn't always as successful as that introduction makes me seem. Once I didn't get a job because they carefully considered my resume and decided I wasn't qualified to have a resume.

■ I'll be speaking about recycling. It's the same speech I gave last year.

■ I'm not going to stand up here and tell you a lot of meaningless things you've heard before. I'm going to tell you some new meaningless things.

■ I'm sure you'd all like to have a few words with the person who scheduled such an early meeting. Unfortunately, he's home asleep.

■ I'm your first speaker. They asked me to come out and break the ice. (pause) Isn't that what the *Titanic* tried to do?

■ I've been told there is magic in my speeches - in fact, sometimes I make entire audiences disappear.

■ If you enjoyed *Dances With Wolves,* you'll love our next speaker – (_____) *Dances With Salesmen.*

■ If you have any questions, please save them until I have some answers.

■ If you're ever in Disneyworld, be sure to visit Florida.

■ It's going to be a long evening – I hope you all have catastrophic boredom insurance.

■ It's great to be here tonight. As Shirley MacLaine

would say: "I'm having the time of my lives."

- Meetings tend to start and finish the same. A clergyman stands at the lectern. The audience is silent with heads bowed and eyes closed. Three hours later, with the featured speaker still standing at the lectern – the audience is silent with heads bowed and eyes closed.

- My flight was so bumpy that when the flight attendant said: "Your lunch will be coming up shortly," she didn't know how right she was.

- Nero had six fierce lions ready for a good show. Lions approached a Christian, who whispered in the lion's ear — and the lion would slink away. Nero told the Christian that he would give him his freedom if he told him what he said to the lions. Christian said he told them that they would be expected to say a few words after dinner.

- Nice audience. Last time, my audience was outstanding – out standing in the lobby.

- Nobody's perfect – which brings us to our next guest.

- Not nervous? Then what were you doing in the ladies room?

- Opening lines: Astrologer – My stars; Obstetrician – You're kidding!

- Please save your questions until after my talk. If you save enough, you can trade them for valuable prizes on your way out.

- Purpose of this meeting is to address problems and make decisions that will affect our company for years to come. Frankly, I would feel better if I hadn't spent five minutes in the buffet line watching one of our executives trying to decide between fruit loops and corn flakes

■ Shortest meeting ever. Sgt-at-Arms said there was a Winnebago blocking the driveway. One member stood and said: "I'll move the Winnebago." Another said: "I'll second that" – The chairman said: "The Winnebago has been moved and seconded. All those in favor say Aye." The vote was unanimous and a minute later the meeting was adjourned.

■ Sorry I'm late, but it takes Marge forever to change a flat.

■ Speakers should keep in mind that within every listener there's a yawn waiting to get out.

■ Thank you for that unexpected sitting ovation.

■ Thank you for that wonderful introduction. After the program, will you help me update my resume?

■ Thanks for the great introduction. I just hope you weren't under oath.

■ That was a great introduction. I can hardly wait to hear myself.

■ The meal was better than a dinner last week — that made me feel good to know that Secretariat didn't die in vain.

■ The role of a speaker is like a body at an Irish wake. It's necessary to have one, but nobody expects you to say much.

■ The theory of relativity also applies to the perceived length of a boring speech. It all depends on whether you are the borer or the boree.

■ There's a first time for everything. I wonder who said that the first time.

■ This will be a great city if they ever get through building it.

■ (Unexpected) As you just heard, we've fnally got our act together. I just didn't know I was going to be given a speaking part.

■ Wait a minute, 1996! I'm not ready yet.

■ We have an extensive program tonight. If you are an insomniac, this might be your lucky night.

■ We have some exciting impromptu events planned for this evening.

■ What can you say about (_____) that hasn't been said about other emperors?

■ William Henry Harrison's inaugural address (8,578 words) was the longest ever. He read it on a cold, raw day and refused to wear a hat or coat. He caught pneumonia and died one month later. The lesson from that bit of history has not been lost on this speaker. I will remain dressed. And I promise you, my speech will be appropriately concise.

■ You're an average American if... you were raised Protestant and believe in God and afterlife, though you didn't go to church last week... you think you will live to be 78... you've named your son Michael and your daughter Jennifer... you charge about $2200 worth of goods a year to your credit cards... you spend 32 percent of the workday goofing off, for a total of

fours months of extra paid vacation a year… you have
at least one house pet, and the chances are 50-50
that you carry a picture of the pet in your wallet…your
household writes about 17 checks a month…you
drive the urban interstate at an average of 58.6
mph…you think spouse-beating is a greater sin than
spying for a foreign country; parking in a handicapped
zone is worse than lying to Congress; and smoking
cigarettes is worse than producing X-rated
videotapes…you're a woman and spend $396 a year
on clothes and wear high heels regularly, even though
they give you foot problems…you're a man and spend
just over $228 a year on clothes and let your wife
buy all your underwear…you eat 1.6 bushels of pop-
corn each year…you consider yourself average looking or better.

■ (When you have to lower the microphone) This must
have been set for a Democrat (or Republican). They're
not as big as they used to be.

Philosophy

■ A good scare is worth more to a person than good advice.

■ A man does not know what he is saying until he knows what he is not saying.

■ A river is like intelligence, the deeper it is the less noise it makes.

■ A rolling stone gathers no moss, and a closed mouth gathers no foot.

■ A slip of the foot you may soon recover from, but a slip of the tongue you may never get over.

■ Cannibals listened with the greatest interest to everything he (the missionary) had to say... and then they ate him. - *Mark Twain*

■ Cheer up, things could be worse. So he cheered up, and things got worse.

■ Confused. Man standing in the pasture holding a piece of hemp in his hands and saying to himself: "I can't remember if I have lost a horse or found a rope."

■ Do not let what you cannot do interfere with what you can do.

■ Don't let yesterday take up too much of today. - *Will Rogers*

■ Never kick a man when he's up.

■ Good examples have twice the value of good advice.

- Home is not where you live, but where they understand you.
- Hope for the best. Expect the worst. Life is a play. We're unrehearsed.
- I have not much patience with a thing of beauty that must be explained to be understood. If it does need added interpretation by someone other than the creator, then I question whether it has fulfilled its purpose. – *Charlie Chaplin*
- If there's one thing we should let others find out for themselves, it's how great we are.
- If you want an accounting of your worth, count your friends.
- It has occurred to me that a man need know but two sentences to survive. The first is how to ask for food.
- It's better to understand a little than to misunderstand a lot.
- It's never too late to be what you might have been.
- Man: Why doesn't this bull have horns? Farmer: Several reasons. Some bulls are born without horns. Some bulls get their horns late in life. Other bulls are dehorned. The main reason why this bull doesn't have horns is that he's a horse.
- Many know how to flatter; few understand how to give praises. – *Greek proverb*
- Mark Twain was asked where he would like to spend the afterlife. He replied: "Heaven for the climate, Hell for the company."
- Mixed emotions is watching your mother-in-law drive

off a cliff in your car.

■ My indecision is final!

■ Our eyes are where they are for seeing opportunities ahead — not for looking at all of our mistakes behind.

■ Proverb. By rushing, you pass by much more than you catch up with. — *American Proverb*

■ Proverb. Even a small star shines in the darkness. - *Finnish proverb*

■ Proverb. If you want your dreams to come true, don't sleep. – *Yiddish proverb*

■ Proverb. That which is brief, if it be good, is good twice over. - *Spanish proverb*

■ Proverb. Treat your guest as a guest for two days. On the third day, give him a hoe. – *Swahili proverb*

■ Proverb. With time and patience the mulberry leaf becomes a silk gown. - *Chinese proverb*

■ Dumb Proverbs: Do not give a man a fish, but teach him to bowl... Most dogs bark but few wear pearls... A candle that stands in water cannot burn at both ends... A dog may bark but his legs will never grow longer... A house without a roof is better than a roof without a house... Guilt doesn't mean you're not to blame.

■ The great advantage of my education is that it didn't interfere with any plans I had for my future. — *Fred Allen*

■ The farther backwards you can look, the farther forward you are likely to see. — *Winston Churchill*

- The man who moves a mountain begins by carrying away small stones. — *Chinese Proverb*
- The person on the top of the mountain didn't fall there!
- There are no shortcuts to any place worth going.
- There are three ingredients in the good life: learning, earning and yearning.
- They made tomorrow so we don't have to do everything today.
- Things always balance out: when someone gets something for nothing, someone else gets nothing for something.
- Treat your friends like family and your family like friends.
- Watch your thoughts, they become words; watch your words they become habits; Watch your habits; they become character.
- We come into this world crying while those all around us are smiling. May we live so that we go out of this world smiling while everyone around us is weeping.
- We make a living by what we get, but we make a life by what we give.
- What other people do, we always feel we could do better.
- Irish toast: May you have the hindsight to know where you've been, the foresight to know where you're going and the insight to know when you're going too far.

A Republican is a Democrat who won the lottery.

Politics

■ Let's put principle aside and do what's right.

■ "Glad you've seen the light." "No. I felt the heat."

■ "I am running as a favorite son." Voice: "That's the greatest unfinished sentence in American politics."

■ "The poorhouse is vanishing among us." – *Herbert Hoover*, Aug. 11, 1928 (just before the stock market crash of 1929.)

■ ... A well-known public serpent.

■ 1996 is another big election year — when we start off

with the Super Bowl and end up with Super Bull.

■ A bureaucrat is a Democrat who holds some office that a Republican wants.

■ A conservative is someone who believes in reform. But not now.

■ A debate is when both candidates pledge their allegiance to TV and to the cameras for which they stand – one notion – indescribable – with promises and goodies for all.

■ A politician is a person who gets sworn in and cursed out.

■ A recent survey indicated that 75% of all Americans couldn't name the presidential candidates. The remaining 25%, of course, ARE the presidential candidates.

■ A sure sign of bureaucracy is when the first person who answers the phone can't help you.

■ Abe Lincoln when called "two faced," said to audience: "If I had another face to wear, do you think I would wear this one?"

■ After seeing all those fires in L.A., I think I'm finally beginning to understand what President Bush meant by "a thousand points of light."

■ America is where anyone can become president. To become a Supreme Court justice – not so easy.

■ An exciting smell coming out of the White House is the smell of broccoli cooking.

■ Any politician will tell you that you can fool all of the people some of the time and some of the people all of the time and usually that's enough.

- As I understand Glasnost, we still have enemies but they're friendly.
- Bill Clinton chose a running mate who is his intellectual equal. George Bush did the same thing.
- Blank bumper sticker for people who are undecided.
- Bureaucracy is the art of making the possible impossible.
- Bush being picketed by a vegetable rights group called GreenPeas.
- Dole or Clinton: Do you want vanilla or vanilla?
- Bush's first budget — stealth tax increase.
- Clinton speech was for the State of the I.O.Union address.
- Campaigning can be tiring. One politician was so frazzled, he kissed my hand and shook my baby.
- Candidates are people who tell you everything they know – and then keep talking.
- Christmas is always an exciting time for politicians. Whenever someone mentions a star in the east, (candidate) thinks they're talking about him.
- Columbus didn't know where he was going, had a potentially mutinous crew and was entirely dependent on borrowed money. Today he'd be a candidate.
- Conservative-liberal — I'm all for a change — but you go first.
- Conservatives have just come out with chastity seat belts for people who fool around in cars.

- Democratic poll on which candidate they would support and a potted plant came in third.
- Do you realize that the principal reason we think Mario Cuomo is smart enough to be president - is that he says he doesn't want to be president?
- Don't think the Mayor has a sense of humor. All I did was two jokes about him and the next day they put in a new tow away zone. My driveway.
- Election Day problem: how to separate the chaff from the chaff.
- Election Day special – turkey stuffed with baloney.
- Election year dilemma: How do you make the right choice between the wrong candidates.
- Ever get the feeling that our city fathers are unmarried.
- Fascinating to watch Hillary Clinton when Bill is making a speech. You can barely see her lips move.
- Foreign aid usually is when poor people of a rich nation send their money to the rich people of a poor nation.
- George Bush said he created over 100,000 small businesses. He doesn't say that before he took office those were 10,000 large corporations.
- Guns don't kill people… bullets fired from guns kill people.
- He's a born politician. His first words were "no comment."
- He's bright, articulate, imaginative, dedicated and sincere. How did he ever get into Congress?

- He's the type who shakes your hand before an election and your confidence after.
- How can you vote a straight ticket and keep a straight face at the same time.
- How George Bush could call himself the "education president," when his only contribution to literacy is a book written by his dog.
- How does it feel to be a woman prime minister? I don't know. I've never been a man prime minister.
- How far would Moses have gone if he had taken a poll in Egypt. – *Harry Truman*
- How many questions needed to get Dan Quayle's attention? Please repeat the question.
- I don't worry about politicians who are accused of misconduct, I worry about those that haven't been caught.
- I have lived in this town all my life. In this town there are 55 bars. And I am proud to say that I have never been in one of them. A voice from the back: "And which one is that?"
- I just can't picture Abraham Lincoln standing outside a factory gate waiting to shake hands with the day shift.
- I know how I am going to vote — very carefully.
- I know why politicians are misunderstood so often. It's not easy to talk and say nothing at the same time.
- I love the way the Disney studio combines live action with cartoon characters. I think they use Congress as a role model.

- I must follow the people. Am I not their leader? – *Disraeli*
- I went to hear a panel of politicians speak. Why do they call it a political *forum* when most of us are *againstum*.
- I won't say how the senators and congressmen got their last pay raise but when they endorse their checks, they wipe their fingerprints off the pen.
- I've come to the conclusion that I will never be President of the United States — and boy, is that a relief!
- If God intended us to have a strong third party, Noah would have taken three of every creature.
- If pro is the opposite of con, what is the opposite of progress? Congress.
- If you can't convince them, confuse them. – *Harry Truman*
- In an election year, it's hard to believe there were only two jackasses aboard Noah's Ark.
- In politics, if you want anything said, ask a man. If you want anything done, ask a woman. — *Margaret Thatcher*
- Iran-Contra hearings cost $10 million. Who said talk was cheap.
- Is it too late to see if Mario Cuomo is still interested?
- It would be really interesting if a candidate took a week off from campaigning to dig into the private lives of reporters.
- It's beginning to look like some of the candidates are having second thoughts. Others still seem to be try-

ing to come up with a first.

■ It's not that the wrong man wins, but the wrong men run.

■ It's true that hard work never killed anybody, but I figure why take the chance. – *Ronald Reagan*

■ Its very hard to pick presidential timber from a forest of balsa wood.

■ Jackie Mason: Comedians should stay out of politics — but then who'd be left to run the country?

■ Just went to my doctor about the problem I'm having with fatigue. It's 1996 and I'm already tired of the presidential campaign.

■ Let he who is without sin among you, contact the Democratic National Committee immediately.

■ Behind every great man is a woman — and reporters trying to find her.

■ Liberals worry about the criminals; the conservatives, the victims.

■ Madonna's book, *SEX,* had as many positions as Bill Clinton's views on a political issue.

■ Many an office holder is sworn in one year and sworn at the next.

■ Many Congressmen are unhappy because they are underpaid, underappreciated and under investigation.

■ Many years ago, George Washington said: "I cannot tell a lie." And ever since, the government kept looking around for someone who could.

■ Mario Cuomo would have made a great quarterback. You never know if he going to run or pass.

- Most political speeches are 50-50 propositions. The politician speaks for 50 minutes. The audience listens for 50 seconds.
- Never try to lie to Congress or Congressmen. Those people are experts in the field.
- Not sure where the Persian Gulf is – but I do know it's closer than it used to be.
- One of the biggest problems facing America today is solid waste. And speaking of solid waste, did any of you watch the debates?
- Our speaker has no equal when it comes to pursuit of the vote. Whenever one of his constituents gets married or has a baby, he sends them a bouquet of flowers. Whenever one of them dies, he sends them an absentee ballot.
- Pantomime is the ancient art of communicating without saying anything. It's a little like political speeches.
- Party platform — gang plank.
- Pat Schroeder cried when she said she wouldn't run for president. I cried when I considered who is.
- Politician was asked if his vote could be bought. "No, but it can be rented."
- Politicians are those who promise you a rose garden and then sell you their seeds.
- Politicians pass the buck — but they hold on to the tens and twenties.
- Politics is the art of looking for trouble, finding it everywhere, diagnosing it incorrectly and applying the wrong remedies. — *Groucho Marx*

- Politics is the gentle art of getting votes from the poor and campaign funds from the rich, by promising to protect each from the other.
- Pollster: Do you believe two key issues we face are ignorance and apathy. Voter: I don't know and I don't care.
- While in office, President Bush sent massive food shipments to the Soviet Union. Most of it is broccoli.
- Private sector workers use the weekend to rest up for the coming week. Civil servants use the week to rest up for the weekend.
- Protecting the boss — Poindexterity.
- Reagan took naps. Bush caused them. Clinton did both.
- (Congressman _____)will be in a new Godfather movie. The Godfather makes him an offer he can't remember.
- Remember the good old days when a covert operation was adjusting your shorts.
- Ross Perot's motto: A mind is a terrible thing to make up.
- Since a politician never believes what he says, he is surprised when others believe him.
- Somehow it seems appropriate that the most famous landmark in Washington, D.C., is a gigantic shaft.
- Summer is difficult time for a Vice President. How does he know when he is on vacation.
- Sure there is lying and double-dealing and deception and guile and evasion and duplicity and deceit and

chicanery and subterfuge and financial hanky-panky.
But nobody's perfect.

■ (Congressman _____) may throw his pants in the ring.

■ No justice in this world. The (baseball team) are called losers because they can't score and (_____), because he could.

■ (_____) supporters were caught stuffing the ballot boxes – with the opposition candidates.

■ My 8-year-old didn't have a costume for a Halloween Party, so he wore his school clothes and went as (_____).

■ Man to (President candidate): "I wouldn't vote for you if you were St. Peter!" (Candidate): "If I were St. Peter, you wouldn't be in my district."

■ If (candidate) is the hope of tomorrow – wake me the day after.

■ I firmly believe that (_____) is just as honest as his fellow Congressman — and that's what worries me.

■ It was a great debate. There was only one low blow when (_____) claimed that everything he said was going over (_____) head.

■ (_____) stirred up apathy all over the country.

■ Woman said: I've slept with (_____). When? Everytime he gives a speech.

■ The candidates in my district are such a joke, our voting booths have a laugh track.

■ The only hope for the Democrats in 1996 — is the Republicans.

- The politicians are three weeks ahead in their speaking and the voters are four weeks behind in their listening.
- The town was so backward that they even voted for Calvin Coolidge. And that was last year.
- The trouble with political jokes is that very often they get elected. – *Will Rogers*
- There is something you can do about junk mail. Write to your congressman and tell him to stop sending it.
- There's a big difference between a President with a vision of the future and one who's just far out.
- This country has come to feel the same when Congress is in session as when the baby gets hold of a hammer. — *Will Rogers*
- Three greatest problems in the world today: Europe, arms control. India, birth control. California, self-control.
- Took oath of office. Wiped fingerprints off Bible.
- Under communism, you have to wait 15 years to buy a car. With capitalism, you can have one immediately, but it takes 15 years to pay it off.
- I want to be buried in Louisiana so I can remain active in politics.
- We all have to pay for our mistakes. Of course, Congress gets them at a volume discount.
- We are developing a whole new generation that thinks running for president is a great way to meet girls.
- We're getting close to turkey day. Not Thanksgiving; election day!

- When a politician says he or she is middle of the road, keep in mind, so are potholes.
- *Who's Who in Politics* is printed in pencil.
- Wiretapping: Called a friend for drink. Tweny-two people showed up.
- Wise old political saying: As Iowa goes, so goes Iowa.
- You can't fool all the people all the time, but it isn't necessary. A majority will do.
- You can't fool all the people all the time. Thats why we have a two-party system. — *Mark Twain*
- Your lips tell me No, No. But there's Yes, Yes, in your lies.
- A politician visited an Indian reservation. Everytime he said anything the chief said "Ado." He wondered what it meant until he was leaving and noticed horse droppings and the Chief said, "Don't step in the Ado."
- Thomas Nast, a political cartoonist for *Harper's Magazine*, first used the images of the donkey and elephant to symbolize the political parties.

Puns

- Did you read the book on... modesty? – Read it? I wrote it!... procrastination? – Not yet... paranoia? — Why do you ask?
- George Callup – inventor of the telephone poll.
- How many astronauts to make a space flight? One to pilot, one to navigate and one to run the Roto-Rooter.
- Millard Fallmore - looks like clumsier U.S. presidents.
- Moses - patriarch told by God to take two tablets and call him in the morning.
- Rin Tin Tan - tanning oil for yuppie puppy.
- Sir Reginald, a portly knight, had saved King Richard's life on the field of battle. In appreciation, the king offered the knight either a huge assortment of luscious pastries or the hand of his daughter, Edith, in marriage. When Sir Reginald hesitated, the king barked, "Make up your mind. You can't have cake and Edith too.
- The Don Rickles Doll. Wind it up and it bites you.
- The mail is in the Czech.
- They are avoided like: Spends most of their time at the cashbar in Algiers... We had a parting of the waves... One letter is worth a thousand words... All's well that ends swell... He's a wolf in cheap clothing... The chickens are coming home to roast... Love is

never having to say your story... All work and no pay makes Jack a dull boy... A fool and his monkey are soon parted... I went to the school of Fort Knox... I'm caught between a rug and a hard place... Have a nice stay... A loaf of bread, a jug of wine and wow... All's fear in love and war.

■ Unappealing products: Pig Newtons (The cookie made from Pork)... Raising fire ants for fun and profit... Using Clam Cough Drops...- Reading the Complete Book of Parasites... The breakfast cereal shaped like spiders.

Retire

■ A bunch of us took up a collection — to buy new locks so you can't get back in.

■ A retirement dinner is when everybody says such nice things about you – if you had heard them all along, you wouldn't have retired.

■ Custom Service man retired. His co-workers confiscated a lovely gold watch for him.

- Eat? We're talking about a man who would have asked for seconds at the Last Supper.
- One retired person has enthusiasm for 30 minutes – another has it for 30 days, but it is the person that has it for 30 years who makes a success in life.
- Give you a gold watch when you no longer have anything to be on time for.
- He brought out the best in people. Or maybe they just look good compared to him.
- He doesn't get a whole lot of mail. Most people prefer attacking him in person.
- He felt his parents wanted a pet; not him. He got that feeling from little things – like the way they always put newspaper on the bottom of his playpen.
- He gave up farming when his wife ran away with the scarecrow.
- He grew up to be the kind of person his parents told him not to hang around with.
- He has reached new heights – not to mention new widths.
- He never called in sick a day in his life. He was out sick many times but he never called in.
- He promised his employees that he would reduce their taxes by 50 percent — he cut their salaries in half.
- He told his wife he felt old, fat, bald, useless and neglected. She said she didn't see why he felt neglected.
- He's a completely different person away from work. He's even been known to make some intelligent decisions.

- He's a man of many gifts – unfortunately, none of them have been unwrapped yet.
- Hope you are enjoying your party; we're deducting the cost from your pension.
- I want to thank you all for coming out tonight to help me celebrate my retirement. But now, if you don't mind, I'm going to leave early, go home and get into bed and get a good nights rest — because tomorrow's my first day of work at McDonald's.
- I've reached that stage in life where if I want to meet women my own age, I hang around the Dr. Scholl's display.
- If I had my life to live over again, I'd start much earlier, and end up much later.
- Left because of "illness and fatigue." His boss was sick and tired of him.
- Much has been written and said about (name) and he's here tonight to deny it.
- NASA is scaling back on expenses. With Chuck's retirement, instead of giving him a watch, they just told him the time.
- Now that I'm retired, I'm still kicking — but I'm not raising much dust.
- One of our company's most laid-back personalities. Just last week he was placed under scrutiny for bizarre, unusual and suspicious behavior. He was seen at his desk — working.
- Our guest has really been around. In fact, there's no end to the number of places he's no longer welcome.

- President announced his retirement. General Manager called every day to ask if it was true. President said: "Don't you believe me?" "Yes, but I like to hear you say it."
- Retired and still calls in sick.
- Retirement is that time when your mind is in first class and your body is in tourist.
- Retirement is the first day of the best of your life.
- Retirement is the good time I've been training for all of my life.
- Retirement is when you bend over to pick something up and wonder who lowered the floor.
- Retirement is when you go from the fast lane to memory lane.
- Retirement is when you look forward to taking up new hobbies, like collecting stamps — food stamps.
- Retirement is when you realize there is life after prune juice.
- Retirement is when you're not dead yet, but you have many of the symptoms.
- Retirement is when you're not dead yet – but you have all the symptoms.
- Retirement is when your main exercise is golf – miniature golf – with a caddy.
- Retirement will produce some big changes in his life. For starters, he'll have to get used to taking his afternoon naps at home.
- Rich? He got into real estate in the days when it was still called dirt.

- Taking early retirement — the only time in his 30 years with the company he has been early.
- The older we are, the greater we were.
- There are signs that tell you when you're getting near to retirement – like when you go to a convention and you are a lot more interested in where the rest room is than where the bar is.
- There is a name for that period of time when you finally have all the skills, experience and know-how your job requires. It's called retirement.
- They say that when you retire you should keep busy and be productive. But why change now?
- This company will never find another employee like (_____). At least that's what we keep hoping.
- This office just won't be the same without you. It will be... what's the word I'm looking for?... productive.
- We are all proud of you. You have given this company the best minutes of your life.
- We passed the hat to buy you a gift. Not only didn't we raise any money, but someone stole the hat.
- We're here tonight to honor a man whom we all know — but we're going to honor anyway.
- What will it take to fill this man's shoes? Well – for starters, socks.
- When he first started, a fax machine was carbon paper, an envelope and a three cent stamp.
- When he joined the company 30 years ago, he came to us with the firm conviction that you can learn from your mistakes — and he's been cramming ever since.

- When I retire, I don't think there will be any government money left for me. Like many others, I suffer from Social Insecurity.
- When there was a problem, we always knew we could come to you and ask what you did to cause it.
- When you don't care where your wife goes as long as you don't have to go along.
- When you wonder how you ever had time to go to work.
- Why is it that when you retire, and time is no longer a matter of urgent importance, your colleagues give you a watch?
- You know you are getting old when it's about time to hang it all up and you can't even remember where you left most of it.
- You made us laugh...you made us cry – but enough about your work.
- You never let us down – since we never expected much from you.
- You wonder who will fill your vacancy and you find out you didn't leave one.
- You've all said such nice things about me, so I've decided to stay.
- Your accomplishments are legendary. For instance, there's the legend of the four-hour workday, the legend of the three-hour lunch, the legend of the astronomical expense report..

Religions

- A real atheist is someone who doesn't even believe in Bingo.
- An enterprising clergyman has opened chain of churches called "Mr. Godwrench."
- Better to limp all the way to heaven than not get there at all.
- Bishop Sheen was lost on his way to the town hall. He asked some kids. They asked why he was going there. Bishop said he was going to tell people how to get to heaven. A boy said: "If you can't get to the Town Hall, how you going to get to heaven?"
- Boy trying to ring doorbell. A Priest stopped to help, and rang the bell. The Priest then said: "What now?" The little boy said: "Run like hell."
- Child saying alphabet. I'm praying but can't think of the right words so I just say all the letters. God will put them together for me because he knows what I'm thinking.
- Comment to the Pope. "Next time bring the Mrs."
- Her dog was killed and she wanted a fine burial for him. She went to the Methodist minister who said he was sorry, but he didn't bury pets. The Episcopal clergy said the same thing. She talked to a Catholic priest who started to say no, but she pleaded – I'll make a donation to the church. Would $1,000 be enough? "Dear lady," said the priest, "why didn't you

tell me your dog was Catholic?"

- Don't know why Sinead O'Connor is mad at the Pope. The person she should be mad at is her barber.
- A little girl had been praying for a pony for weeks without results. Finally one night she took her statute of the Virgin Mary, put it in a box under her bed and wrote the following letter: Dear God, if you ever want to see your mother again..."
- Jim Bakker faces 120 years in jail — but he'll probably get time off for odd behavior.
- Man sleeping in church. The Preacher asked those who want to go to heaven to stand. Man sleeps. Preacher said: "Who wants to go to hell (loudly)." Man stands: "Don't know what we are voting for but you and I are the only ones standing."
- Men become priests because they are not tough enough to be nuns.
- My friend is half-Hindu and half-Catholic. She goes around with a bingo marker in the middle of her forehead.
- Moses came down from the mountain and said: "I got Him down to 10 but He still wants adultery on the list."
- Old lady to minister: "Sorry to see you go. I never knew what sin was until you came here."
- One church now has an Express Confession - for people with eight sins or less.
- Our church has needed a new roof and a new preacher ever since the old roof fell on the old preacher.

- Sin, lust, desire, intrigue. If that doesn't bring people back to religion, nothing will.
- There is a religious group in one country that stops and prays in the middle of the street. They are called Moslems. In America, if a person stops and prays in the middle of the street, they are called casualties.
- Three Lutheran pastors invited by Catholic priest to attend Mass. They arrived late and had to stand in back of church. Priest whispered to one of altar boys, "Get three chairs for our Lutheran friends." Boy didn't hear so priest said louder, "Three chairs for the Lutherans." Altar boy stepped to the altar rail and called out: Three cheers for the Lutherans!"
- What a blast if an archaeological expedition went up to Mount Sinai and found one more tablet that said: "Disregard previous commandments."
- What do you call a Nun sleepwalker? A roaming Catholic.
- What do you say to an atheist when he sneezes?
- What does Tammy Bakker put on for Halloween?
- Where does God live? In my bathroom. Every morning my Dad shouts, "My God, are you still in there?"
- Who would have thought that what started in a manger would have ended up in a mansion.
- With all the talk about shredders, it's good that God gave us the Ten Commandments on two tablets of stone.
- Woman apologized to minister about her husband walking out during the sermon. It's not a reflection

on you. He has walked in his sleep ever since he was a child.

■ World was created by God in six days and on the seventh day, He rested. Then on the eighth day, He started to answer the complaints.

■ School kids were drawing. One boy was making a picture of God. The teacher said no one knows what he looks like. The little boy said: "They will in a minute."

Buy small cars to make your house look bigger.

Small

- 7-11 closes at 6 p.m.
- As Lemuel Gulliver said to the Lilliput store manager, "Don't you have anything in my size?"
- Dinosaurs are proof that big isn't necessarily better.
- Fire Department offered same day service.
- From where I stand – and I am standing...
- I want you all to understand that I'm not short, I'm just vertically impaired.
- I wouldn't be the first person you'd choose to lead a standing ovation.
- It doesn't depend on size or a cow could catch a rabbit. — *Penn. Dutch Proverb*

- It is easy to dodge an elephant but not a fly.
- It's better to have loved a short girl than never to have loved a tall.
- It's said that what he lacks in size, he makes up in quickness.
- Life is too short to be little.
- Mickey Rooney just came out with his autobiography. It was a short story.
- One street in town and it's one way.
- The dinosaur's eloquent lesson is that some bigness is good but an overabundance of bigness is not necessarily better.
- The town was so small that the First National Bank was a guy with big pockets.
- To belittle is to be little.
- What counts is not the size of a dog in a Fight. It's the fight in the dog. — *Dwight Eisenhower*

Sexy

- A girl called me to go out one time. I told her I would. Then I had a problem. The girl was my boss' wife.
- Doctors say you can definitely enjoy sex after ninety, but it's a good idea to let someone else drive.
- Girl told her date that she didn't know him enough to dance the Lambada with him – so they had sex instead.
- He told me he worked with diamonds and later I found out that he was a baseball umpire.
- I like to date school teachers. You kiss them once and they make you do it over and over again until you get it right
- I'm not opposed to sex education in the schools, but I have to draw the line when they begin dispensing Snoopy diaphragms.
- Kids are too young to get sex education in the school. What do they know about headaches.
- Last night I hung up in the middle of an obscene phone call — I just couldn't think of anything more to say.
- I told my son about the birds and the bees. He told me about my wife and the butcher. – *Rodney*

Dangerfield

■ On a trip to a zoo. A teacher took a group of children to see the monkeys. The monkeys were not in the cages and the teacher asked the attendant where they were. He said the monkeys were mating behind the cage. The teacher said: "Offer some peanuts! Tempt them to come out." The attendant said: "Would you?"

■ The Marines want just a few good men. I had an aunt like that.

■ The Personnel Department had to revise its employment applications. They found that where it says "SEX: M or F." Some people thought it meant "Moderate" or "Frequent."

■ Teenagers are people who think sex was invented in 1979.

Roast

- Allow me to introduce the greatest thing since Sominex.
- Before bringing out our next speaker, I'd just like to mention that this concludes the coherent part of today's program.
- Earned a special place in this company — and can go there as soon as the janitor is through cleaning the stalls.
- Five years ago he was just a nobody. Today he's five years older.
- He is a man who really believes in the American Dream. Every time he gives a speech he puts people to sleep.
- He brightens up a conversation when he stops talking.
- He comes from such a small town, his address was "Bob."
- He had a lot more to say but always tries to observe the first rule of public speaking: "Nice guys finish fast." He's not fast.
- He has been called conceited, arrogant, insensitive, domineering – and a mother should know.
- He has reached the stage where his narrow waist and

broad mind have switched places.
- He invented the can opener. But it was a complete failure. Nobody had invented the can yet.
- He is someone who appreciates the fact that you're only young once. He just can't remember when that was.
- He wanted to marry the girl next door but unfortunately he lived next door to a brothel.
- He was recently given a 21-gun salute...unfortunately they missed.
- He wears a cologne called "Kielbasa."
- He's a man of few words, but repeats them over and over and again.
- He's like a son to me — the one I threw out of the house.
- He's not the brightest person. He keeps a set of spare car keys locked in the truck.
- He's so vain, he joined the Navy so the world could seen him.
- Her latest book recently went into its second printing. Now there are two copies.
- His company wanted to make him an associate, but no one would associate with him.
- His friends threw him a surprise party. I was surprised to hear he had friends.
- In high school he was voted as most likely to settle out of court.
- Our guest is to this industry what broccoli is to George Bush.

- Plastic surgery wouldn't help his looks, but plastic explosives might.
- Put a seashell to his ear and got a busy signal.
- The last time he had an original thought it died of loneliness.
- The only reason he's not famous is that no one has ever heard of him.
- We are pleased our guest was able to make it tonight. You know how fickle parole boards can be.
- We came to praise Chuck, not to bury him. But the vote was close.
- Well respected? She's often quoted by people who don't want to appear too intelligent.
- When they made this guy, they not only threw away the mold – they burned down the foundry.

Songs

■ All black and blue is Mr. O'Grady. He read by braille a tattooed lady.

■ As I put a record on the old Victrola, she dropped a mickey in my Pepsi-Cola.

■ Don't put those towels in the suitcase Mother. There's lots more room in the trunk.

■ Grandpa, lend me your upper plate, I want to put the bite on a friend.

■ Her boyfriend stole her only brassiere and then he left her flat.

■ I've stopped making love to that girl in the bank, I just found out she's a teller.

■ She was only a grease monkey's daughter which explained why she liked to get oiled.

Sports

■ A dedicated golfer is one who can't understand how a hooker can be happy.

■ A new coach hired to revive a losing team said: "We are going back to basics, to the beginning. Forget everything you have learned about football." Then he held up a football and said: "Guys, this is a football." One of the players said: "Not so fast."

■ A quick way to meet new people is to pick up the wrong ball on a golf course.

■ Arguing with the umpire has never won a ball game.

What's the biggest challenge for a skier?
Getting through revolving doors.

But it has helped lose many.

- A hunter lies in wait. A Fisherman waits and lies.
- Bad when the team carries off the coach and fumbles him.
- Baseball manager went to Heaven. God gave him one wish. So he picked a team of baseball greats. The Devil challenged that team to a game. The manager said: "We have all the great players." Satan said: "We have all the umpires."
- Boxer told interviewer: "Millions of people will see me fight tonight," he boasted. Interviewer said: "And every one of them will know the results "about 10 seconds before you do."
- Charley Esper was a pitcher in the 1890s for Baltimore. Because he ran like a lame horse, his teammates called him "Charley Horse."
- Coach asked why his team lost. He said: There are 28 teams and every week, 12 got to win and 12 got to lose.
- Difference between a .250 hitter and a .300 hitter is one more hit every 20 times up.
- Football quarterbacks have a real problem with public speaking. They are not used to looking people in the eye.
- Golf courses originally designed with varying numbers of holes, depending on the parcel of land. St. Andrews originally had 22 holes but in 1764, the number was reduced to 18 – and became the standard.

■ Golf is a game that requires a large amount of territory to provide its players with a small amount of exercise that costs a maximum amount of money and gives a minimum amount of satisfaction.

■ Golf is like a love affair: If you don't take it seriously, it's no fun; if you do take it seriously, it breaks your heart.

■ Golf is the only activity in which finishing *under* par is considered a great success.

■ Golfer fell in the lake but his playing partners kept on walking as he thrashed about in the water. Another player said: "Aren't you going to help him. He'll drown." One friend said: "Naahh. He can't keep his head down long enough."

■ Golfer in Hades was overjoyed at the beautiful course; grabbed a set of clubs and asked Satan where the golf balls were. Satan said we have not a one — that's the Hell of it.

■ Hockey: A form of disorderly conduct, with scores.

■ Horse placed a bet on himself to win. The cashier was not impressed. The horse came back to cash in the winning ticket and asked the cashier if he was surprised that he could talk. No, but I never thought you'd win.

■ I hate golf because it isn't a contact sport – I never make contact with the ball.

■ I just found out why prehistoric men beat one another with clubs. They had to because hockey had not been invented.

■ I never lost a game. I just ran out of time.

■ If basketball had never been invented, where would all the high school dances be held.

■ If God had truly meant for us to have dominion over the earth and all the living creatures upon it – He never would have given us the Baltimore Orioles.

■ Leo Durocher was coaching first base when the Giants were playing an exhibition at West Point. A Cadet kept shouting: How did you get into the major leagues? Leo said: My Congressman appointed me.

■ Lou Holk, asst. to Woody Hayes when O.J. Simpson ran 87 yards for a touchdown. At halftime, Woody yelled at Lou "Why did he run 87 yards for a TD?" Holtz said: "That's all he needed."

■ My golf pro told me how I could cut 12 strokes off my score – skip one Par 3.

■ My golf pro told me to keep my head down, so I did – and somebody stole my golf cart.

■ Nothing increases your golf score like witnesses.

■ Old golfers, settle up after every hole.

■ One advantage of bowling over golf is that you very seldom lose a bowling ball. - *Don Carter*

■ One thing about camping and the great outdoors: It makes you appreciate even more the great indoors.

■ Said he was a diamond cutter. He mowed the grass at the ball park.

■ Secretariat, the champion race horse, spent the last 15 years of his life as a stud. Needless to say, he died smiling.

- Swimsuit issue. Don't know why they put those women in a sports magazine – most men can't get to first base with them.
- Skiing is the sport that conquers your fear of height by giving you so many other things to worry about.
- So many sports teams are named after Indians: The Chiefs, The Redskins, The Braves... Maybe that's where the term "ticket scalping" comes from.
- Some parents take Little League too seriously. One couple was so disappointed with their son's playing, they traded him to another family.
- Some team! They won the toss and elected to go home.
- Sportsmanship is to be able to win as if it were a matter of course and to lose as if it were a pleasant change.
- The team played so miserably, the people at the stadium shouted, "Up in front."
- The trouble with being a good sport is that you have to lose in order to prove it.
- The will to win is important, but it isn't worth a nickel unless you also have the will to prepare.
- There is a connection between pain and pleasure. So it makes perfect sense that *golf* spelled backwards is *flog*.
- We bow our heads on Sunday. Some of us are praying and some of us are putting.
- Winning isn't everything, but it beats coming in second. – *Bear Bryant.*

Truisms

- Dog couldn't catch a rabbit. The rabbit was running for his life and the dog just running for his dinner.
- Don't go around saying the world owes you a living. The world owes you nothing. It was here first. – *Mark Twain*
- A day of worry is more exhausting than a week of work.
- A duty is a task we look forward to with distaste, perform with reluctance, and brag about afterwards.
- A lie can travel halfway around the world while the truth is putting on its shoes. – *Mark Twain*
- A lot of good people are too busy trying to get ahead to do a good job.
- A lot of people die at 40, but they are not buried until 30 years later.
- A meeting is no substitute for progress.
- A person always has two reasons for doing anything — a good reason and the real reason.
- A telephone book is full of facts but doesn't contain a single idea.
- Almost every idea is good sometime.
- Always strive to tell the truth, even if you have to make it up.

■ America did not invent human rights. Human rights invented America. – *Jimmy Carter* in farewell address

■ An English scientist, Sir Humphry Davy, invented the electric light? TRUE. Thomas Edison was the first to design a lamp filament good enough to be marketed. Humphry Davy, 77 years earlier, was the first to make a wire glow by sending electricity through it.

■ Anyone can hold the helm when the sea is calm. - *Publilius Syrus*

■ Arriving 15 minutes early does nothing but guarantee a 30-minute wait.

■ As obedient as a shadow...as fickle as a weathervane...as relaxed as empty gloves.

■ As they say about nuclear war, "You've seen one, you've seen them all."

■ Behind every successful man, you'll find somebody who says: "I went to school with him." - *Earl Wilson*

■ Better to ask twice than to lose your way once. - *Danish proverb*

■ Big companies are small companies that have succeeded.

■ Borrow trouble for yourself but don't lend it to your neighbors. - *Rudyard Kipling*

■ Character is much easier kept than recovered.

■ Compromise is not always the best solution. Imagine two negotiators facing each other on opposite cliffs. It would do them little good to meet half-way.

■ Do more than belong, participate... Do more than care, help... Do more than believe, practice... Do more than be fair, be kind... Do more than forgive, forget... Do more than dream, work. — *William Arthur Ward*

■ Don't ask the barber whether you need a haircrut.

■ Don't ask... Are you asleep?... Now what's the matter?... Have I kept you waiting?... You don't remember me, do you?... Will you promise not to get mad if I ask you something?

■ Don't be humble. You're not that great.

■ Don't ever take a fence down until you know the reason why it was put up.

■ Don't get too big for your britches; you're sure to be exposed in the end.

■ Easy doesn't do it.

■ Every leader needs to look back once in a while to make sure he has followers.

■ Every silver lining has a cloud.

■ Everybody loves success but they hate successful people. - *John McEnroe*

■ Everybody wants to go to heaven but nobody wants to die. - *Joe Louis*

■ Everyone seems to know what his "rights" are. Wouldn't it be terrific if we also knew what our "wrongs" were?

■ Everything looks impossible for the people who never try anything.

■ Everywhere is walking distance if you have the time. – *Steven Wright*

■ Facts...22,000 checks will be deducted from the wrong

234

bank accounts in the next 60 minutes... 12 babies will be given to the wrong parents each day... 3,056 copies of tomorrow's *Wall Street Journal* will be missing one of three sections... 18,322 pieces of mail will be handled in the next hour... 114,500 mismatched pairs of shoes will be shipped this year... 315 entries in *Webster's Third New International Dictionary of the English Language* will turn out to be misspelled.

■ Few things are more upsetting than getting a second opinion that you like less than the first.

■ Find an aim in life before you run out of ammunition.

■ Flattery should be treated like chewing gum, enjoy it for a short while, but don't swallow it.

■ Fools rush in – and get all the best seats.

■ Freedom. People demand freedom of speech to make up for the freedom of thought which they avoid.

■ Friendship is like a bank account. You can't continue to draw on it without making deposits.

■ From misfortune to fortune is a long way. From fortune to misfortune is but a step. — *Yiddish Proverb*

■ George Washington was the first president of the United States? False. John Hanson of Maryland served as the first "president of the United States in congress assembled" in 1781-2 under the Articles of Confederation.

■ Hand guns are only dangerous when they're loaded - So are most drivers.

■ He who hesitates is sometimes saved.

■ History repeats itself because each generation refused

to read the minutes of the last meeting.

- I am easily satisfied with the best. – *Winston Churchill*
- If it feels good, do it. It's the things that feel great that you have to worry about.
- If it is to be, it is up to me.
- If it weren't for the last minute, nothing would get done.
- If someone asks you if you're indecisive, don't respond with "Well, yes and no."
- If the shoe fits, you're lucky.
- If you can't get people to listen to you any other way, tell them it's confidential.
- If you do not think about the future, you will not have one.
- If you don't care where you are, you're not lost.
- If you don't learn anything from your mistakes there's no sense in making them.
- If you have always done it that way, It is probably wrong. Like Smokey The Bear.
- If you lose the power to laugh, you lose the power to think.
- If you put off doing an easy job, it only makes it harder. If you put off doing a hard job it makes it impossible.
- If you tinker with something long enough, eventually it will break.
- If you want an accounting of your worth, count your friends.
- If you're yearning for the good old days, just turn off the air conditioning.

- In our haste to deal with the things that are wrong, let us not upset the things that are right.
- In 1914, the first year income tax was collected, Americans paid an average per capita tax of 41 cents – and only one percent of the population was obligated to pay taxes at all.
- It is better to have one person working with you than having three people working for you. — *Dwight Eisenhower*
- It is much easier to be critical than to be correct. - *Benjamin Disraeli*
- It is not enough to stare up the steps — you must step up the stairs.
- It's always easier to forgive an enemy after you have gotten even.
- It's easier to do a job right than to explain why you didn't.
- Just about the time most of us finally learn all the answers,they change the questions.
- Just when you think you have someone eating out of your hand, count your fingers.
- Lincoln's Emancipation Proclamation freed the slaves immediately? FALSE. The proclamation applied only to the Confederacy and was not legal until Union forces gained control.
- Live so that you wouldn't be ashamed to sell the family parrot to the town gossip. – *Will Rogers*
- Live so that your friends can defend you but never have to.

- Many of us spend half of our time wishing for things we could have if we didn't spend half of our time wishing.
- Measure twice and saw once.
- Misfortune is a point of view. To an aspirin salesman, your headache feels terrific.
- Mother whale to offspring: "When you are spouting, you are most likely to be harpooned."
- Nero fiddled while Rome burned? FALSE. Contrary to legend, Nero didn't start the fire or cavort with a violin - an instrument that didn't appear in Italy for another 1,500 years.
- Never argue with a fool... He may be doing the same thing.
- Never explain – your friends do not need it and your enemies will not believe you anyway.
- Never get into fights with ugly people because they have nothing to lose.
- Never hire a plumber who wears rubber boots or an electrician with scorched eyebrows.
- Never insult an alligator until you've crossed the river.
- Never invite a pyromaniac to a house-warming party.
- No matter how much a person dreads the future, he or she usually wants to be around to see it.
- No matter what goes wrong, there's always someone who knew it would.
- No one is ever too old to learn a new way to do something dumb.
- Nobody wants to hear about your labor pains. They

only want to see the baby.

■ None of us are as strong as all of us.

■ Nothing is quite so annoying as to have someone go right on talking when you're interrupting.

■ Nothing makes a person more productive than the last minute.

■ Nothing seems to keep a plane on time so much as your arriving at the airport a little late.

■ Nothing will give you more free time than being punctual.

■ Nothing will improve a person's hearing more than praise.

■ Once I make up my mind, I'm full of indecision.

■ One moment of patience may ward off a great disaster; one moment of impatience may ruin a whole life.

■ One nice thing about silence is that it can't be repeated.

■ One reason I don't drink is that I want to know when I'm having a good time. - *Mae West*

■ Outside of traffic, there is nothing that has held this country back as much as committees. — *Will Rogers*

■ People may doubt what you say, but they will believe what you do.

■ People who drive at excessive speeds usually get where they're going ahead of time - sometimes thirty or forty years.

■ People who live in glass houses shouldn't do much of anything.

■ People who cannot find time for recreation are obliged

sooner or later to find time for illness.

- Presence is more than just being there.
- Professionals built the Titanic — amateurs built the Ark.
- Proverb: In difficulty, you understand your friends. – *Chinese proverb*
- Proverb: Many know how to flatter; few understand how to give praise — *Greek proverb*
- Proverb: People count up the faults of those who keep them waiting. – *French proverb*
- Proverb: Too humble is half proud. — *Yiddish proverb*
- Public opinion is held in reverence. It settles everything. Some think it is the voice of God. - *Mark Twain*
- Quantity is what you can count. Quality is what you can count on.
- Reason it is so difficult to make ends meet is because someone is always moving the ends.
- Remember, an orchestra conductor's baton in the wrong hands is just a stick.
- Rule of thumb in the Stock Market: Those who say, don't know, and those who know, don't say.
- Solved problems have simple answers.
- Some people are so busy learning the tricks of the trade that they don't learn the trade.
- Some people never miss an opportunity to miss an opportunity.
- Some people never hear opportunity knock because they're too busy knocking opportunity.

■ Some people will believe anything if you whisper it to them.

■ Someday is not a day of the week.

■ Taxi drivers always go that extra mile.

■ The best remedy for a short temper is a long walk.

■ The best safety device in a car is a rearview mirror with a police officer in it.

■ The biggest disappointments come to those who get what's coming to them.

■ The Declaration of Independence was signed on July 4,1776? FALSE. July 4 was the day the Declaration was adopted by the Second Continental Congress. It was signed on August 2.

■ The discovery of the North Pole revealed that there is nobody sitting on top of the world.

■ The future is not something we enter. The future is something we create.

■ The great music concert of 1969 was held in Woodstock, NY.? FALSE. It was held on a farm near Bethel, N.Y., more than 40 miles from Woodstock, the town originally intended as the site.

■ The higher you climb the flagpole, the more people see your rear end.

■ The minority is always wrong - at the beginning.

■ The next best thing to a lie is a true story nobody will believe. — *Mark Twain*

■ The people most preoccupied with titles and status are usually the least deserving of them.

■ The quickest way to find a lost item is to buy another

just like it.

- The reason most people have a clean conscience is because they never use it.
- The surest time to be late is to have plenty of time.
- There are two sides to every argument... until you take one.
- There is no speed limit on the pursuit of excellence.
- Think twice before calling yourself an expert. "Ex" is a has been. "Spurt" is a big drip under pressure.
- Three of the most diffcult things to do in life are to keep a secret, forget an injury, and make good use of leisure time.
- Time is what we want most but what we use worst. — *William Penn*
- Too many people are so busy being good that they don't have time to be excellent.
- True fame is when you dominate the conversation... after you've left the room.
- Vacation is when people load up the kids and the camera so they can drive 500 miles to take a picture of the family standing in front of the car.
- Vince Lombardi didn't become a head coach in the NFL until he was 47. Eddie Arcaro lost his first 45 races. Michael Jordan was cut from his high school basketball team. It's not how you start; it's how you finish.
- We are always doing something for posterity, but just once I would like to see posterity do something for us. – *Joseph Addison* (1672-1719)

- We are damned not for doing wrong but for not doing right. - *Robert Louis Stevenson*
- We don't see things as they are, we see things as we are. – *Anais Nin*, French-born American novelist
- We find it difficult to distinguish our needs from our greed.
- We have to learn to be our own best friends because we fall too easily into the trap of being our worst enemies.
- We judge ourselves by what we feel capable of doing, while others judge us by what we have already done. — *Henry Wadsworth Longfellow*
- We never get a second chance to make a first impression.
- What we learn from the past is that we seldom learn from the past.
- When the only tool you have is a hammer, everything begins to look like a nail.
- Why is it... that the easiest way to do anything is wrong?... that the scales in the doctor's office always weighs several pounds more than your own?... that the newspapers you spread on the floor to catch paint spills are such fascinating reading?... that people who are great at remembering a joke can't remember how many times they've already told it to you?
- World's oldest profession – cave cleaning.
- You won't strain your eyes if you look at the bright side of things.
- You've got to be good before you can do good. - *Aldous Huxley*

Television

■ I discovered an alternative to Network Programming and Cable Programming. It's called the OFF knob.

■ I love all these new TV programs. They give me time to catch up on my reading.

■ If God had meant for man to sit and watch TV he would not have given us a brain.

■ If you have any doubt of life after death, just watch the reruns of TV programs that were canceled.

■ Television is a medium because it's neither rare or well done. - *Ernie Kovacs*

■ Television is something we watch in order to tell other people why we don't.

■ There is an educational channel on your TV. You can find it by turning your knob to the position marked OFF.

■ TV Programs: MY TWO HEADS - A teen with an unusual handicap. Tonight, Eric receives two hats as a birthday present. WIDE WORLD OF SHORTS - Men of all ages parade around in their undies before judges.

■ Watching C-span shortens one's Attention-Span.

■ What bothers me about TV is that it tends to take our minds off our minds.

■ The reason why television is called a medium is because nothing on it is ever well done. – *Fred Allen*

■ Who says TV is not educational. It teaches us that there are better things to do than watching television.

What Did You Say?

- Our comedies are not to be laughed at." You've got to take the sour with the bitter." "We are dealing with facts, not reality." – *Sam Goldwyn*
- Anyone who goes to see a psychiatrist ought to have his head examined. – *Samuel Goldwyn*
- Anyone who favors capital punishment should be shot.
- Avoid making the wrong mistakes. — *Yogi Berra*
- Chicago Mayor Richard Daley — What keeps people apart is their inability to get together.
- Give me a ball-point estimate.
- He was caught between a rock and a hot plate.
- He's beginning to throw a monkey in the wrench.
- I don't want to get my neck out on a limb on this one.
- I used to be a hypochondriac, but then I got sick of it.
- I'll have to give them mouth-to-mouth resurrection.
- If that happens, we'll be accused of blue murder.
- It's selling like cupcakes.
- That's private only for your consummation.
- This is one of those explosive items where I see red flags.
- This is the earliest I've ever been late. – *Yogi Berra*
- You can observe a lot just by watching. – *Yogi Berra*
- Tux with contraband around the waist.
- You have got to be able to take the thunder out of our sails.
- You have to hear between the lines.

Well, Well, Well

- A friend gave me the phone number of a terrific diet center. In just one week, I lost the phone number.
- Another friend said about a great speaker that he would rather hear him speak than eat A voice replied from the audience: "So would I. I've heard him eat."
- After an exhaustive multi-million dollar health study, the government concluded that people would live longer if they didn't die sooner.
- Caveman said: "Everything we eat is 100% natural, yet our life expectancy is only 27 years."
- Developing a birth control pill for men. So far, so good. None of the male volunteers have gotten pregnant.
- Diet — a plan of putting off tomorrow what you put on today.
- Diet is the penalty you pay for exceeding the feed limit.
- Dieting – the triumph of mind over platter.
- Does this dress make me look fat? "No. It's your thighs that make you look fat."
- Drug habits are supporting drug cartels. Eating habits are supporting grocery cartels.
- Good plan to lose weight — a two-week vacation in

Somalia.
- He looks like the reason for world famine.
- I accidentally played my workout tape in reverse — and gained weight.
- I asked my doctor how my body compared to other men my age. He asked: "Living or deceased?"
- I eliminated sugar, fat and salt from my new diet — then I eliminated the diet.
- I once tried dieting. It was the worst three hours of my life.
- I see the light at the end of the refrigerator.
- I used to watch golf and baseball on TV, but my doctor said I needed to get more exercise. So now I watch hockey.
- I went to a bachelor party for a health nut. A girl jumped out of a rice cake.
- I'm a firm believer of the benefits of exercise. That's why I set aside 30 minutes a day to think about it.
- I'm on one of those liquid shake diets. I have a shake for breakfast, a shake for lunch and then a sensible dinner – a sensible steak, sensible French fries, sensible beer, some sensible pie, etc.
- It would be unhealthy for me to stop smoking. The only excerise I get is running to the store for a pack.
- It's meals like that, that give food a bad name.
- It's not the minutes at the table that makes him fat, it's the seconds.
- Meals like that could start a new trend – praying after meals.

■ Most diets let you eat all you want of anything you don't like.

■ Most stretch pants have no other choice.

■ My compliments to the chef: that's the first time I can remember having coffee, steak and ice cream — all at the same temperature.

■ Orson Wells on dieting: "My doctor has advised me to give up those intimate little dinners for four...unless there are three other people eating with me.

■ Wife's ex-husband is suing for palimony. I think he's entitled to some of her money – after all, he struck with her through thick and thicker.

■ Sales clerk to customer: "These stretch pants come with a warranty of one year or 500,000 calories – whichever comes first."

■ She looks like a crowd coming down the street.

■ That was a meal fit for a king. King is the name of my dog.

■ That was the kind of food mother used to make. That is just one reason dad and I left home.

■ The hardest part of dieting is not watching what you eat – it's watching what other people eat.

■ The only way to keep your health is to eat what you don't want, drink what you don't like and do what you'd rather not.

■ To tell you the truth, my idea of vigorous exercise is eating faster.

■ We do a lot of exercising that we don't need to: we jump to conclusions, run down our friends, dodge issues, push our luck, walk out on people, swing until the wee hours and try to climb the social ladder. It's ok if we jog our memories, hike up our pants, kick bad habits, hit the sack early, score well on a test, punch the time clock, dive into our work, strike a nerve, shoot the bull or pass the time.

■ Went to fancy diet clinic. In just 10 days, I lost $5,000.

■ What an appetite! At our last meeting he ate the pie chart.

■ So much rain that animals in the zoos are beginning to line up in pairs.

"Vince Spezzano is really spaced out — his jokes are from another planet! (They're out of this world.)"

...Former Astronaut Alan Shepard Jr., RADM USN (ret.)

ZZZ - I'm Friend Vince

■ I've come to this conclusion. It's one I've long supposed. The boss's door is open. It's his mind that's always closed.